YOUR PERSONAL
HOROSCOPE
2009

♌

LEO

YOUR PERSONAL
HOROSCOPE
2009

LEO

23rd July–23rd August

igloo

igloo

This edition published by Igloo Books Ltd,
Cottage Farm, Sywell, Northants NN6 0BJ
www.igloo-books.com

Produced for Igloo Books by W. Foulsham & Co. Ltd,
The Publishing House, Bennetts Close, Cippenham,
Slough, Berkshire SL1 5AP, England

ISBN: 978-1-84817-059-9

This is an abridged version of material
originally published in *Old Moore's Horoscope
and Astral Diary*.

Printed and manufactured in China

CONTENTS

INTRODUCTION

Your Personal Horoscopes have been specifically created to allow you to get the most from astrological patterns and the way they have a bearing on not only your zodiac sign, but nuances within it. Using the diary section of the book you can read about the influences and possibilities of each and every day of the year. It will be possible for you to see when you are likely to be cheerful and happy or those times when your nature is in retreat and you will be more circumspect. The diary will help to give you a feel for the specific 'cycles' of astrology and the way they can subtly change your day-to-day life. For example, when you see the sign ☿, this means that the planet Mercury is retrograde at that time. Retrograde means it appears to be running backwards through the zodiac. Such a happening has a significant effect on communication skills, but this is only one small aspect of how the Personal Horoscope can help you.

With Your Personal Horoscope the story doesn't end with the diary pages. It includes simple ways for you to work out the zodiac sign the Moon occupied at the time of your birth, and what this means for your personality. In addition, if you know the time of day you were born, it is possible to discover your Ascendant, yet another important guide to your personal make-up and potential.

Many readers are interested in relationships and in knowing how well they get on with people of other astrological signs. You might also be interested in the way you appear to very different sorts of individuals. If you are such a person, the section on Venus will be of particular interest. Despite the rapidly changing position of this planet, you can work out your Venus sign, and learn what bearing it will have on your life.

Using Your Personal Horoscope you can travel on one of the most fascinating and rewarding journeys that anyone can take – the journey to a better realisation of self.

THE ESSENCE
OF LEO

Exploring the Personality of Leo the Lion

(23RD JULY – 23RD AUGUST)

What's in a sign?

What really sets you apart from the herd is your naturally cheerful tendencies and your ability to display a noble and very brave face to the world at large. Leos are big people, no matter what their physical size may be and it is clear that you could never be an 'also-ran'. Quite the reverse is usually the case because you are at the forefront of many ventures, ideas and enterprises.

Being a Leo brings quite a few responsibilities. For example, people tend to look up to you, which means you have to be on your best behaviour for a lot of the time. Not that this prevents you from showing a slightly mischievous face to the world on a regular basis. You are not given to worrying too much because you generally know how to get yourself out of any sort of difficulty with ease. It's true that you tend to face problems head-on – a natural extension of your rather courageous temperament. Sometimes this can get you into unnecessary scrapes, as can your tendency to pit yourself against the forces of nature, or social groups that you feel to be absolutely wrong in their intentions or objectives.

As a Leo you do recognise that you have a responsibility to others, particularly those types who are shyer than you, or individuals who just don't have the ability to look after themselves. With a smile and a shrug you are inclined to put a protecting arm around the whole world. In effect you are the perfect big brother or sister and take pride in the position you tend to gain in society. In a work sense you are capable and can very easily find yourself in a situation of responsibility. You don't worry about this and can make a fine executive in almost any profession. There's no doubt though that you are naturally best placed at the head of things.

♌

It's true that you are inclined to do too much and that your levels of energy are far from inexhaustible. However, it's a love of life that counts for the most in your case, and nothing is going to prevent you from being the happy, sunny, freewheeling soul that represents the sign of Leo at its very best.

Leo resources

Your ruling planet is the Sun, the source of all heat, light and therefore life on the Earth. The Sun is fundamental to our very existence, and its primary importance at the centre of things is reflected in your nature. Unlike your brother sign, Aries, you display your Fire-sign tendencies in a more controlled manner and without the need to dominate to such a great extent. All the same your natural position is at the head of things and this is reflected in the resources you draw from the zodiac.

One of your greatest gifts is a natural tendency to look confident, even on those occasions when you might be quaking inside. It's amazing what a difference this makes because it more or less ensures that others will trust you and tend to follow your lead. Once they do you rise to the occasion in an admirable way because you don't want to let your followers down. In almost any situation that life could present, you will quite naturally take charge, and those around you are invariably happy that it should be so.

Most Leos are capable in a practical as well as a theoretical way but a hands-on approach probably works best. Leo leads from the front, which means having to keep fit and healthy. This is vital, but like the lion that your sign represents you can get rather lethargic and flabby if you don't keep in shape. Also like the lion you do have a tendency to appear lazy on occasions, but only usually when things are already running smoothly around you.

The professions chosen by Leos are many and varied. It isn't really the subject matter that is important, merely your ability to make an impression. At work, as well as in social situations, you can shine like the very Sun that rules you. Usually well liked and respected, you are in a position to utilise the popularity that comes your way in order to feather your own nest, as well as those of people around you. Domestically speaking you have a great love of home and family, though you might tend to stifle those you love a little on occasions.

Beneath the surface

'What really makes me tick?' A fair question, and one that members of many zodiac signs are constantly inclined to ask themselves – but not you. The fact is that you are not the deepest thinker around. This is not to suggest that you don't have lofty ideals or a very sound moral base to your behaviour. The reason that you probably are not one of life's natural philosophers is because you are a 'doer'. In the time it takes others to mull over any given situation you will have sorted it out and moved on to the next task. However, this is a natural skill that can be honed to perfection and depends in part on getting yourself interested in the first place.

Your boredom threshold tends to be quite low and you would soon feel fatigued if you were forced to remain in situations which meant doing the same thing time and time again. Your driving, sometimes impatient mentality does demand change, and you can become irritable and out of sorts if you don't find it.

Are you as confident as you often appear to be? The answer to that one has to be yes. The fact is that you quite often fail to bear in mind the possibility of failure. Of course this means that you are more disappointed than most when things do go wrong, but your very conviction often leads to success. Once you do get down in the dumps however, you can be a very sorry picture indeed. Fortunately, you have the mental and spiritual reserves to pick yourself up fairly quickly and to push forward once again.

In matters of love you are probably more reserved than you give the impression of being. All the same you know how to deal with relationships – that is until you start acting like a lion again. The over-protective quality of your animal sign is always a danger, and one that you need to control. Perhaps here we find the Achilles heel of Leo. It is quite common for you to experience a sense of jealousy, a fact that would make you more possessive than usual. You have to remember that it's fine to love, but impossible to 'own' another individual.

In the main you offer the world an exterior smile that reflects your genuine inner state. Truthfulness shows on your face, and is usually felt in your heart in equal proportion.

Making the best of yourself

To feel good and to make the right sort of impression, you have to look good too. Nobody goes to the safari park to see a moth-eaten lion. You can dress cheaply, but you have to cut a dash in some way. Drab colours definitely don't suit your personality, with bright oranges and yellows being the most favoured – a reflection of your Sun rulership. Once you are properly attired you tend to move forward positively through life. Most Leos are quite attractive people, mainly because the honesty, frankness and genuine courage of your personality has a habit of finding its way to the surface.

There is one line of Kipling's famous poem 'If' that springs to mind as an object lesson for Leo, this being 'And yet don't look too good, nor talk too wise'. It is quite possible for you to go over the top in your enthusiasm and even courage isn't same thing as foolhardiness. A little humility can go a long way, as can a determination to learn from people who know better than you do. Constantly knocking your head against the same brick wall isn't very productive, and can sometimes be avoided by simply showing a willingness to take advice. And it isn't as if people are unwilling to lend a hand. The Leo subjects who achieve the most in life have learned how to co-operate, though without feeling that they are having to relinquish the leading position in life that is so important to them.

In order for you truly to make the best of yourself you also need to be fit. Leos are inclined to have some problems associated with the heart and the circulatory system, so you need to exercise regularly and to avoid the sort of constant stress that can lead to longer-term health difficulties. To most Leos laughter is the best tonic of all.

The impressions you give

If we could all genuinely see ourselves as others see us, how much easier would be our interaction with the world at large? Yours may not be the most intuitive sign of the zodiac but you are perceptive enough to know when you are giving the right impression. If this fact is sometimes obscured it is at least easy for you to monitor when things are not going right. In turn this should result in a slight modification of your own personality to take account of circumstances.

If you have any specific problem in this direction it stems from the fact that you are not a natural philosopher. Doing is far more important than thinking to you, a truism that can sometimes be your downfall. More attention to detail and a better appraisal of others allow you to offer a much better impression of yourself.

Most people already find you sunny, warm, frank, free, delightfully outspoken and very brave. All you have to do to achieve real success is to build on the qualities you already possess and to make allowance for the fact that the world is full of individuals. You can't browbeat others into liking you, even though popularity is important to you. There will always be people who don't take to your personality and there really isn't much you can do about the situation.

A great advantage for you is that it isn't difficult for you to appear to know what you are talking about, even when you don't. You can gain extra skills on the way and should use the very real magnetism of your personality both to help the world and to improve your own situation. Few people would find you easy either to dismiss or to forget, which can be another very definite advantage in life.

A sense of proportion is sometimes important, as well as a defined purpose in your statements and actions. All in all you have most of the components that allow you to be popular. Build on these and your true Leo worth will be there for all to see.

The way forward

No sign of the zodiac typifies its planetary ruler more than your own sign of Leo. When you smile, the Sun comes out and your laughter is so infectious that even the hardest-hearted types would be likely to smile themselves. Add to this the fact that you typify the statement 'fools rush in where angels fear to tread' and you have a formidable combination at your disposal. It might be the case that you fail to take account of some of your actions, but a good-humoured and intelligent attitude to life also allows you to get out of scrapes as easily as you get into them.

Cultivate your tendency to stick up for the underdog and don't get yourself into a position in life that means you constantly have to pay lip service to people who clearly don't know what they are doing. You can't stand incompetence, arrogance, cruelty or oppression. Of course this is a fine attitude, but you can't put the world right on your own, so once again co-operation proves to be the key to success.

In a career sense you need to be doing something that constantly stretches you. Your boredom threshold is not high and with constant tedium can come a worrisome streak and a tendency to health difficulties. Variety in work is the spice of your life, together with an active and useful social life, which is also vitally important.

In matters of love you are sincere and ardent, though with a tendency towards being a little too possessive. Allowing others the freedom to go their own way means finding more happiness yourself and lifts the noble qualities of your nature to new heights. Leos are still more likely than people from other zodiac signs to find one important relationship in life and to stick with it. Part of the reason for this state of affairs is that you have a horror of failure and will persist, even when others fall by the wayside.

You may not be creative in the generally accepted sense of the word but you have a good eye for colour and enjoy cheerful surroundings. Practical and capable, you won't need to call on the services of experts too often, since Leos generally don't shy away from DIY chores.

Diet is vitally important because as a Leo you are inclined to put on weight readily. Exercise helps here and is something you revel in anyway. Use your natural talents to the full, defend the weak and fight oppressors and you can't go far wrong in your life. Most important of all, keep smiling. You are tremendous fun to have around.

LEO ON THE CUSP

Astrological profiles are altered for those people born at either the beginning or the end of a zodiac sign, or, more properly, on the cusps of a sign. In the case of Leo this would be on the 23rd of July and for two or three days after, and similarly at the end of the sign, probably from the 21st to the 23rd of August.

The Cancer Cusp – July 23rd to July 25th

You tend to take life at a slower pace than Leo when taken on its own. You are more sensitive and quieter by nature, with slightly less drive and enthusiasm and a less dynamic disposition. With a creative and generally aspiring nature, you draw from Leo the fearless qualities that are typical of the sign, but these only tend to show on those occasions when you feel very strongly about things. There is quite a contradiction between these two signs and therefore you have a tendency to show very different faces in different circumstances. This fact makes you slightly awkward to predict and you often shock people as a result. Just when the world thinks it has you pigeon-holed, off you go at a tangent, perplexing your relatives and friends all over again. Family members are very important to you and when your aspiring and lofty qualities show most it is often on their behalf. In matters of love you tend to be very loyal, and have the ability to mix very well with others, enjoying cheerful and original people as part of your social circle.

One area that needs particular attention is your health. Although generally more robust than you probably give yourself credit for, you get through a tremendous amount of nervous energy, much more than others may realise. You need to watch your diet very carefully and to avoid acidic foods, which can upset your stomach. Apart from this, however, you are virtually indestructible and have the capacity to work long and hard to achieve your objectives.

At work you do your best to be adaptable and are very good at managing others. The natural frustrations of Leo, when faced with opposition, are less accented in your case. You have the ability to get on well and should make a mark for yourself when happy with your lot. Few would find you overbearing or bossy, although at times you seem to lack some of the natural Leo confidence. Most important of all though – you are kind, generous, trusting and very good to know.

The Virgo Cusp – August 21st to August 23rd

Perhaps the greatest difficulty for people born under the influence of this cusp is in making themselves understood. You probably think that you are the least complicated person in the world, but that isn't the way others see you. Your nature is full of contradictions. On the one hand you are fanatically tidy, and yet you can work in a state of almost total chaos; you love to travel and yet, deep inside, you are a home bird; and you talk a great deal, but often with quiet confidence. To disentangle all these contradictions is as difficult for you as it is for anyone else, and so you may often not reach the level of self-confidence that you deserve.

You have most of the positive qualities associated with the zodiac sign of Leo and your lofty, aspiring, sunny disposition is usually well accepted. Beneath this, however, is a quiet and contemplative person, who needs moments alone to synthesise the many happenings in a busy life. Usually physically robust, you do tend to worry more than is good for you, frequently about matters that are not particularly important. Meditation suits you well, particularly the kind that has a physical aspect, as this satisfies your Leo qualities, too. With a nervous system that varies from day to day, it is important for you to be sure that you achieve the level of relaxation that is vital to your Virgoan qualities. For you this could be anything between a crossword puzzle and two weeks on a cruise ship. In social settings you enjoy a degree of variety and can manage quite well with new people, even though you often tend to stick to people with whom you are familiar.

It's always important for you to keep an open mind and you shouldn't allow negative thoughts to build up. Keeping busy makes sense, as long as you don't continually choose to burn the candle at both ends. The people who know you the best do find you difficult to understand, but they are inclined to love you all the more for that. The most important character trait for you to cultivate is optimism because the more cheerful you remain regarding the future, the greater is the effort you expound upon it.

LEO AND ITS ASCENDANTS

The nature of every individual on the planet is composed of the rich variety of zodiac signs and planetary positions that were present at the time of their birth. Your Sun sign, which in your case is Leo, is one of the many factors when it comes to assessing the unique person you are. Probably the most important consideration, other than your Sun sign, is to establish the zodiac sign that was rising over the eastern horizon at the time that you were born. This is your Ascending or Rising sign. Most popular astrology fails to take account of the Ascendant, and yet its importance remains with you from the very moment of your birth, through every day of your life. The Ascendant is evident in the way you approach the world, and so, when meeting a person for the first time, it is this astrological influence that you are most likely to notice first. Our Ascending sign essentially represents what we appear to be, while the Sun sign is what we feel inside ourselves.

The Ascendant also has the potential for modifying our overall nature. For example, if you were born at a time of day when Leo was passing over the eastern horizon (this would be around the time of dawn) then you would be classed as a double Leo. As such, you would typify this zodiac sign, both internally and in your dealings with others. However, if your Ascendant sign turned out to be a Water sign, such as Pisces, there would be a profound alteration of nature, away from the expected qualities of Leo.

One of the reasons why popular astrology often ignores the Ascendant is that it has always been rather difficult to establish. We have found a way to make this possible by devising an easy-to-use table, which you will find on page 157 of this book. Using this, you can establish your Ascendant sign at a glance. You will need to know your rough time of birth, then it is simply a case of following the instructions.

For those readers who have no idea of their time of birth it might be worth allowing a good friend, or perhaps your partner, to read through the section that follows this introduction. Someone who deals with you on a regular basis may easily discover your Ascending sign, even though you could have some difficulty establishing it for yourself. A good understanding of this component of your nature is essential if you want to be aware of that 'other person' who is responsible for the way you make contact

with the world at large. Your Sun sign, Ascendant sign, and the other pointers in this book will, together, allow you a far better understanding of what makes you tick as an individual. Peeling back the different layers of your astrological make-up can be an enlightening experience, and the Ascendant may represent one of the most important layers of all.

Leo with Leo Ascendant

This is a breathless combination! The fact is that you are a go-getter of the first order, and there is virtually nothing in life that would prevent you from getting what you want. The problem here is that once you have it, you probably want something else. All in all you could end up like a dog chasing its own tail and so the first advice is to slow down and enjoy the journey a little more. Not that all of this makes you any less likeable, or indispensable, to a whole host of people. You smile much more often than you scowl and you won't make heavy weather of problems that would rock others back on their heels.

You are rather materialistic, and ultimate success probably means more to you than it should, but you can easily stop on your hectic journey to take note of those who have fallen by the wayside and give them a helping hand. If all that power is used for the good of humanity you might even become a living saint, except for the fact that you would be too busy to accept the honour. Be careful that you don't weigh yourself down with so many responsibilities that you fail to notice your progress, and travel as much as you can because this will certainly broaden your mind. Most people find you very attractive and fun to have around.

Leo with Virgo Ascendant

Here we have cheerfulness allied to efficiency, which can be a very positive combination for most of the time. With all the sense of honour, justice and bravery of the Leo subject, Virgo adds better staying power through tedious situations and offers you a slightly more serious view of life than we would expect from the Lion alone. In almost any situation you can keep going until you get to your chosen destination and you also find the time to reach out to the people who need your unique nature the most. Few would deny your kindness, though you can attract a little envy because it seems as though yours is the sort of personality that everyone else wants.

Most people born with this combination have a radiant smile and will do their utmost to think situations through carefully. If there is any tendency to be foolhardy, it is carefully masked beneath a covering of Virgoan common sense. Family matters are dealt with efficiently and with great love. Some might see you as close one moment and distant the next. The truth is that you are always on the go and have a thousand different things to think about, all at the same time. On the whole your presence is noticed, and you may represent the most loyal friend of them all.

Leo with Libra Ascendant

Libra brings slightly more flexibility to the fixed quality of the Leo nature. On the whole you do not represent a picture that is so very different from other versions of the Lion, though you find more time to smile, enjoy changing your mind a great deal more and have a greater number of casual friends. Few would find you proud or haughty and you retain the common touch that can be so important when it comes to getting on in life generally. At work you like to do something that brings variety, and would probably soon tire of doing the same task over and over again. Many of you are teachers, for you have patience, allied to a stubborn core. This can be an indispensable combination on occasions and is part of the reason for the material success that many folk with this combination achieve.

It isn't often that you get down in the dumps, as there is generally something more important around the next corner and you love the cut and thrust of everyday life. You always manage to stay young at heart, no matter what your age might be, and you revel in the company of interesting and stimulating types. Maybe you should try harder to concentrate on one thing at once and also strive to retain a serious opinion for more than ten minutes at a time, although Leo does help to control any flighty tendencies which show up.

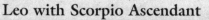

Leo with Scorpio Ascendant

A Leo with intensity, that is what you are. You are committed to good causes and would argue the hind leg off a donkey in defence of your many ideals. If you are not out there saving the planet you could just be at home in the bath, thinking up the next way to save humanity from its own worst excesses. In your own life, although you love little luxuries, you are sparing and frugal, yet generous as can be to those you take to. It's a fact that you don't like everyone and of course the same is true in reverse. It might be easier for you to understand why you dislike others than to appreciate the reverse side of the coin, for your pride can be badly dented on occasions. Scorpio brings a tendency to have down spells, though the fact that Leo is also strongly represented in your nature should prevent them from becoming a regular part of your life.

It is important for you to learn how to forgive and forget, and there isn't much point in bearing a grudge because you are basically too noble to do so. If something goes wrong, kiss the situation goodbye and get on with the next interesting adventure, of which there are many in your life. Stop-start situations sometimes get in the way but there are plenty of people around who would be only too willing to lend a helping hand.

Leo with Sagittarius Ascendant

Above and beyond anything else you are naturally funny, and this is an aspect of your nature that will bring you intact through a whole series of problems that you manage to create for yourself. Chatty, witty, charming, kind and loving, you personify the best qualities of both these signs, whilst also retaining the Fire-sign ability to keep going, long after the rest of the party has gone home to bed. Being great fun to have around, you attract friends in the way that a magnet attracts iron filings. Many of these will be casual connections but there will always be a nucleus of deep, abiding attachments that may stay around you for most of your life.

You don't often suffer from fatigue, but on those occasions when you do there is ample reason to stay still for a while and simply take stock of situations. Routines are not your thing and you like to fill your life with variety. It's important to do certain things right, however, and staying power is something that comes with age, assisted by the fixed quality of Leo. Few would lock horns with you in an argument, which you always have to win. In a way you are a natural debator but you can sometimes carry things too far if you are up against a worthy opponent. Confidence is not lacking and you go with ease through situations that would cause many people to give up.

Leo with Capricorn Ascendant

What really sets you apart is your endless patience and determination to get where you want to go, no matter how long it takes you to do so. On the way there are many sub-plots in your life and a wealth of entertaining situations to keep you amused. Probably somewhat quieter than the average Leo, you still have the capacity to be the life and soul of the party on those occasions when it suits you to be so. Energy, when allied to persistence, is a powerful commodity and you have a great need to take on causes of one sort or another. Probably at your best when defending the rights of the oppressed, you take the protecting qualities of Leo to greater heights than almost anyone else who is touched by the idealistic and regal qualities of the sign. If arguments come into your life, you deal with them quickly and, in the main, wisely. Like most Capricorn types, you take to a few individuals who will play a part in your life for years on end.

Being a good family type, your partner and children are extremely important and you will lavish the same patience, determination and ultimate success on their behalf that you do when dealing with more remote situations. The fact is that you do not know any other way to behave and you are at your best when there is some mountain to climb.

Leo with Aquarius Ascendant

All associations with Aquarius bring originality, and you are no exception. You aspire to do your best most of the time, but manage to achieve your objectives in an infinitely amusing and entertaining way. Not that you set out to do so, because if you are an actor on the stage of life, it seems as though you are a natural one. There is nothing remotely pretentious about your breezy personality or your ability to occupy the centre of any stage. This analogy is quite appropriate because you probably like the theatre. Being in any situation when reality is suspended for a while suits you down to the ground, and in any case you may regularly ask yourself if you even recognise what reality is. Always asking questions, both of yourself and of the world at large, you soldier on relentlessly, though not to the exclusion of having a good time on the way.

Keeping to tried and tested paths is not your way. You are a natural trail-blazer who is full of good ideas and who has the energy to put them into practice. You care deeply for the people who play an important part in your life, but are wise enough to allow them the space they need in order to develop their own personalities along the way. Most people like you, many love you, and one or two think that you are the best thing since sliced bread.

Leo with Pisces Ascendant

You are a very sensitive soul, on occasions too much so for your own good. However, there is no better advocate for the rights of humanity than you, and you constantly do what you can to support the downtrodden and oppressed. Good causes are your thing and there are likely to be many in your life. You will probably find yourself pushed to the front of almost any enterprise of which you are a part because, despite the deeper qualities of Pisces, you are a natural leader. Even on those occasions when it feels as though you lack confidence, you manage to muddle through somehow, and your smile is as broad as the day. Few sign combinations are more loved than this one, mainly because you do not have a malicious bone in your body and will readily forgive and forget, which the Lion on its own often will not.

Although you are capable of acting on impulse, you do so from a deep sense of moral conviction, so that most of your endeavours are designed to suit other people too. They recognise this fact, and will push a great deal of support back in your direction. Even when you come across troubles in your life you manage to find ways to sort them out, and will invariably find something new to smile about on the way. Your sensitivity rating is massive and you can easily be moved to tears.

Leo with Aries Ascendant

Here we come upon a situation in which Leo is allied with another Fire sign. This creates a character that could appear to be typically Aries at first sight and in many ways it is, though there are subtle differences that should not be ignored. Although you have the standard Aries ability for getting things done, many of the tasks you do undertake will be for and on behalf of others. You can be proud, and on some occasions even haughty, and yet you are also regal in your bearing and honest to the point of absurdity. Nobody could doubt your sincerity, and you have the soul of a poet combined with the bravery of a lion.

All of this is good, but it makes you rather difficult to approach, unless the person in question has first adopted a crouching and subservient attitude. Not that you would wish them to do so. It's simply that the impression you give and the motivation that underpins it are two quite different things. You are greatly respected, and in the case of those individuals who know your real nature, you are also deeply loved. But life would be much simpler if you didn't always have to fight the wars that those around you are happy to start. Relaxation is a word you don't really understand and you would be doing yourself a favour if you looked it up in a dictionary.

Leo with Taurus Ascendant

Oh dear, this can be rather a hedonistic combination. The trouble is that Taurus tends to have a great sense of what looks and feels right, whilst Leo, being a Cat, is inclined to preen itself on almost any occasion. The combination tends towards self-love, which is all too likely for someone who is perfect. But don't be too dispirited about these facts, because there is a great deal going for you in other ways. For a start you have one of the warmest hearts to be found anywhere, and you are so brave that others marvel at the courage you display. The mountains that you climb may not be of the large, rocky sort, but you manage to find plenty of pinnacles to scale all the same, and you invariably get to the top.

Routines might bore you a little more than would be the case with Taurus alone, but you don't mind being alone. Why should you? You are probably the nicest person you know! Thus if you were ever to be cast up on a deserted island you would people the place all on your own, and there would never be any crime, untidiness or arguments. Problems only arise when other people are involved. However, in social settings you are charming, good to know and full of ideas that really have legs. You preserve your youth well into middle age but at base you can tend to worry more than is good for you.

Leo with Gemini Ascendant

Many Gemini people think about doing great things, whilst those who enjoy a Leo Sun do much more than simply think. You have the intrepid qualities of Gemini, but you always keep a sense of humour and are especially good to be around. Bold and quite fearless, you are inclined to go where nobody has gone before, no matter if this is into a precarious business venture or up a mountain that has not been previously climbed. It is people such as you who first explored the world, and you love to know what lies around the next corner and over the far hill.

Kind and loving, you are especially loyal to your friends and would do almost anything on their behalf. As a result they show the greatest concern for you too. However, there are times when the Cat walks alone, and you are probably better at being on your own than would often be the case for the typical Gemini subject. In many way you are fairly self-contained and don't tend to get bored too much unless you are forced to do the same things time and time again. You have a great sense of fun, could talk to just about anyone and usually greet the world with a big smile.

Leo with Cancer Ascendant

This can be a very fortunate combination, for when seen at its best it brings all the concern and the natural caring qualities of Cancer, allied to the more dynamic and very brave face of Leo. Somehow there is a great deal of visible energy here but it manifests itself in a way that always shows a concern for the world at large. No matter what charitable works are going on in your district, it is likely that you will be involved in one way or another, and you relish the cut and thrust of life much more than the retiring side of Cancer would seem to do. You are quite capable of walking alone and don't really need the company of others for large chunks of the average day. However, when you are in social situations you fare very well and can usually be observed with a smile on your face.

Conversationally speaking you have sound, considered opinions and often represent the voice of steady wisdom when faced with a situation that calls for arbitration. In fact you will often be put in this situation and there is more than one politician and union representative who shares this undeniably powerful zodiac combination. Like all those associated with the sign of Cancer you love to travel and can make a meal out of your journeys, with brave, intrepid Leo lending a hand in the planning and the doing.

THE MOON AND THE PART IT PLAYS IN YOUR LIFE

In astrology the Moon is probably the single most important heavenly body after the Sun. Its unique position, as partner to the Earth on its journey around the solar system, means that the Moon appears to pass through the signs of the zodiac extremely quickly. The zodiac position of the Moon at the time of your birth plays a great part in personal character and is especially significant in the build-up of your emotional nature.

Your Own Moon Sign

Discovering the position of the Moon at the time of your birth has always been notoriously difficult because tracking the complex zodiac positions of the Moon is not easy. This process has been reduced to three simple stages with our Lunar Tables. A breakdown of the Moon's zodiac positions can be found from page 35 onwards, so that once you know what your Moon Sign is, you can see what part this plays in the overall build-up of your personal character.

If you follow the instructions on the next page you will soon be able to work out exactly what zodiac sign the Moon occupied on the day that you were born and you can then go on to compare the reading for this position with those of your Sun sign and your Ascendant. It is partly the comparison between these three important positions that goes towards making you the unique individual you are.

♌

HOW TO DISCOVER YOUR MOON SIGN

This is a three-stage process. You may need a pen and a piece of paper but if you follow the instructions below the process should only take a minute or so.

STAGE 1 First of all you need to know the Moon Age at the time of your birth. If you look at Moon Table 1, on page 33, you will find all the years between 1911 and 2009 down the left side. Find the year of your birth and then trace across to the right to the month of your birth. Where the two intersect you will find a number. This is the date of the New Moon in the month that you were born. You now need to count forward the number of days between the New Moon and your own birthday. For example, if the New Moon in the month of your birth was shown as being the 6th and you were born on the 20th, your Moon Age Day would be 14. If the New Moon in the month of your birth came after your birthday, you need to count forward from the New Moon in the previous month. If you were born in a Leap Year, remember to count the 29th February. You can tell if your birth year was a Leap Year if the last two digits can be divided by four. Whatever the result, jot this number down so that you do not forget it.

STAGE 2 Take a look at Moon Table 2 on page 34. Down the left hand column look for the date of your birth. Now trace across to the month of your birth. Where the two meet you will find a letter. Copy this letter down alongside your Moon Age Day.

STAGE 3 Moon Table 3 on page 34 will supply you with the zodiac sign the Moon occupied on the day of your birth. Look for your Moon Age Day down the left hand column and then for the letter you found in Stage 2. Where the two converge you will find a zodiac sign and this is the sign occupied by the Moon on the day that you were born.

Your Zodiac Moon Sign Explained

You will find a profile of all zodiac Moon Signs on pages 35 to 38, showing in yet another way how astrology helps to make you into the individual that you are. In each daily entry of the Astral Diary you can find the zodiac position of the Moon for every day of the year. This also allows you to discover your lunar birthdays. Since the Moon passes through all the signs of the zodiac in about a month, you can expect something like twelve lunar birthdays each year. At these times you are likely to be emotionally steady and able to make the sort of decisions that have real, lasting value.

YEAR	JUN	JUL	AUG	YEAR	JUN	JUL	AUG	YEAR	JUN	JUL	AUG
1911	26	25	24	1944	20	20	18	1977	16	16	14
1912	16	15	13	1945	10	9	8	1978	5	5	4
1913	4	3	2/31	1946	29	28	26	1979	24	24	22
1914	23	22	21	1947	18	17	16	1980	13	12	11
1915	12	11	10	1948	7	6	5	1981	2	1/31	29
1916	1/30	30	29	1949	26	25	24	1982	21	20	19
1917	19	18	17	1950	15	15	13	1983	11	10	8
1918	8	8	6	1951	4	4	2	1984	29	28	26
1919	27	27	25	1952	22	22	20	1985	18	17	16
1920	16	15	14	1953	11	11	9	1986	7	7	5
1921	6	5	3	1954	1/30	29	28	1987	26	25	24
1922	25	24	22	1955	20	19	17	1988	14	13	12
1923	14	14	12	1956	8	8	6	1989	3	3	1/31
1924	2	2/31	30	1957	27	27	25	1990	22	22	20
1925	21	20	19	1958	17	16	15	1991	11	11	9
1926	10	9	8	1959	6	6	4	1992	1/30	29	28
1927	29	28	27	1960	24	24	22	1993	20	19	17
1928	18	17	16	1961	13	12	11	1994	9	8	7
1929	7	6	5	1962	2	1/31	30	1995	27	27	26
1930	26	25	24	1963	21	20	19	1996	17	15	14
1931	16	15	13	1964	10	9	7	1997	5	4	3
1932	4	3	2/31	1965	29	28	26	1998	24	23	22
1933	23	22	21	1966	18	17	16	1999	13	13	11
1934	12	11	10	1967	7	7	5	2000	2	1/31	29
1935	1/30	30	29	1968	26	25	24	2001	21	20	19
1936	19	18	17	1969	14	13	12	2002	10	9	8
1937	8	8	6	1970	4	4	2	2003	29	28	27
1938	27	27	25	1971	22	22	20	2004	16	16	15
1939	17	16	15	1972	11	11	9	2005	6	6	4
1940	6	5	4	1973	1/30	29	28	2006	26	25	23
1941	24	24	22	1974	20	19	17	2007	15	15	13
1942	13	13	12	1975	9	9	7	2008	4	3	1/31
1943	2	2	1/30	1976	27	27	25	2009	23	22	20

TABLE 2   MOON TABLE 3

DAY	JUL	AUG	M/D	R	S	T	U	V	W	X
1	R	U	0	CA	CA	LE	LE	LE	LE	VI
2	R	U	1	CA	LE	LE	LE	VI	VI	VI
3	S	V	2	LE	LE	LE	VI	VI	VI	LI
4	S	V	3	LE	LE	VI	VI	VI	LI	LI
5	S	V	4	LE	VI	VI	LI	LI	LI	LI
6	S	V	5	VI	VI	LI	LI	LI	SC	SC
7	S	V	6	VI	LI	LI	LI	SC	SC	SC
8	S	V	7	LI	LI	LI	SC	SC	SA	SA
9	S	V	8	LI	LI	SC	SC	SC	SA	SA
10	S	V	9	SC	SC	SC	SA	SA	SA	SA
11	S	V	10	SC	SC	SA	SA	SA	CP	CP
12	S	V	11	SA	SA	SA	CP	CP	CP	CP
13	T	V	12	SA	SA	SA	CP	CP	AQ	AQ
14	T	W	13	SA	SA	CP	CP	CP	AQ	AQ
15	T	W	14	CP	CP	CP	AQ	AQ	AQ	PI
16	T	W	15	CP	CP	AQ	AQ	AQ	PI	PI
17	T	W	16	AQ	AQ	AQ	AQ	PI	PI	PI
18	T	W	17	AQ	AQ	AQ	PI	PI	PI	AR
19	T	W	18	AQ	AQ	PI	PI	PI	AR	AR
20	T	W	19	PI	PI	PI	PI	AR	AR	AR
21	T	W	20	PI	PI	AR	AR	AR	TA	TA
22	T	W	21	PI	AR	AR	AR	TA	TA	TA
23	T	W	22	AR	AR	AR	TA	TA	TA	GE
24	U	X	23	AR	AR	TA	TA	TA	GE	GE
25	U	X	24	AR	TA	TA	TA	GE	GE	GE
26	U	X	25	TA	TA	GE	GE	GE	CA	CA
27	U	X	26	TA	GE	GE	GE	CA	CA	CA
28	U	X	27	GE	GE	GE	CA	CA	CA	LE
29	U	X	28	GE	GE	CA	CA	CA	LE	LE
30	U	X	29	GE	CA	CA	CA	LE	LE	LE
31	U	X								

AR = Aries, TA = Taurus, GE = Gemini, CA = Cancer, LE = Leo, VI = Virgo, LI = Libra, SC = Scorpio, SA = Sagittarius, CP = Capricorn, AQ = Aquarius, PI = Pisces

MOON SIGNS

Moon in Aries

You have a strong imagination, courage, determination and a desire to do things in your own way and forge your own path through life.

Originality is a key attribute; you are seldom stuck for ideas although your mind is changeable and you could take the time to focus on individual tasks. Often quick-tempered, you take orders from few people and live life at a fast pace. Avoid health problems by taking regular time out for rest and relaxation.

Emotionally, it is important that you talk to those you are closest to and work out your true feelings. Once you discover that people are there to help, there is less necessity for you to do everything yourself.

Moon in Taurus

The Moon in Taurus gives you a courteous and friendly manner, which means you are likely to have many friends.

The good things in life mean a lot to you, as Taurus is an Earth sign that delights in experiences which please the senses. Hence you are probably a lover of good food and drink, which may in turn mean you need to keep an eye on the bathroom scales, especially as looking good is also important to you.

Emotionally you are fairly stable and you stick by your own standards. Taureans do not respond well to change. Intuition also plays an important part in your life.

Moon in Gemini

You have a warm-hearted character, sympathetic and eager to help others. At times reserved, you can also be articulate and chatty: this is part of the paradox of Gemini, which always brings duplicity to the nature. You are interested in current affairs, have a good intellect, and are good company and likely to have many friends. Most of your friends have a high opinion of you and would be ready to defend you should the need arise. However, this is usually unnecessary, as you are quite capable of defending yourself in any verbal confrontation.

Travel is important to your inquisitive mind and you find intellectual stimulus in mixing with people from different cultures. You also gain much from reading, writing and the arts but you do need plenty of rest and relaxation in order to avoid fatigue.

Moon in Cancer

The Moon in Cancer at the time of birth is a fortunate position as Cancer is the Moon's natural home. This means that the qualities of compassion and understanding given by the Moon are especially enhanced in your nature, and you are friendly and sociable and cope well with emotional pressures. You cherish home and family life, and happily do the domestic tasks. Your surroundings are important to you and you hate squalor and filth. You are likely to have a love of music and poetry.

Your basic character, although at times changeable like the Moon itself, depends on symmetry. You aim to make your surroundings comfortable and harmonious, for yourself and those close to you.

Moon in Leo

The best qualities of the Moon and Leo come together to make you warm-hearted, fair, ambitious and self-confident. With good organisational abilities, you invariably rise to a position of responsibility in your chosen career. This is fortunate as you don't enjoy being an 'also-ran' and would rather be an important part of a small organisation than a menial in a large one.

You should be lucky in love, and happy, provided you put in the effort to make a comfortable home for yourself and those close to you. It is likely that you will have a love of pleasure, sport, music and literature. Life brings you many rewards, most of them as a direct result of your own efforts, although you may be luckier than average and ready to make the best of any situation.

Moon in Virgo

You are endowed with good mental abilities and a keen receptive memory, but you are never ostentatious or pretentious. Naturally quite reserved, you still have many friends, especially of the opposite sex. Marital relationships must be discussed carefully and worked at so that they remain harmonious, as personal attachments can be a problem if you do not give them your full attention.

Talented and persevering, you possess artistic qualities and are a good homemaker. Earning your honours through genuine merit, you work long and hard towards your objectives but show little pride in your achievements. Many short journeys will be undertaken in your life.

Moon in Libra

With the Moon in Libra you are naturally popular and make friends easily. People like you, probably more than you realise, you bring fun to a party and are a natural diplomat. For all its good points, Libra is not the most stable of astrological signs and, as a result, your emotions can be a little unstable too. Therefore, although the Moon in Libra is said to be good for love and marriage, your Sun sign and Rising sign will have an important effect on your emotional and loving qualities.

You must remember to relate to others in your decision-making. Co-operation is crucial because Libra represents the 'balance' of life that can only be achieved through harmonious relationships. Conformity is not easy for you because Libra, an Air sign, likes its independence.

Moon in Scorpio

Some people might call you pushy. In fact, all you really want to do is to live life to the full and protect yourself and your family from the pressures of life. Take care to avoid giving the impression of being sarcastic or impulsive and use your energies wisely and constructively.

You have great courage and you invariably achieve your goals by force of personality and sheer effort. You are fond of mystery and are good at predicting the outcome of situations and events. Travel experiences can be beneficial to you.

You may experience problems if you do not take time to examine your motives in a relationship, and also if you allow jealousy, always a feature of Scorpio, to cloud your judgement.

Moon in Sagittarius

The Moon in Sagittarius helps to make you a generous individual with humanitarian qualities and a kind heart. Restlessness may be intrinsic as your mind is seldom still. Perhaps because of this, you have a need for change that could lead you to several major moves during your adult life. You are not afraid to stand your ground when you know your judgement is right, you speak directly and have good intuition.

At work you are quick, efficient and versatile and so you make an ideal employee. You need work to be intellectually demanding and do not enjoy tedious routines.

In relationships, you anger quickly if faced with stupidity or deception, though you are just as quick to forgive and forget. Emotionally, there are times when your heart rules your head.

Moon in Capricorn

The Moon in Capricorn makes you popular and likely to come into the public eye in some way. The watery Moon is not entirely comfortable in the Earth sign of Capricorn and this may lead to some difficulties in the early years of life. An initial lack of creative ability and indecision must be overcome before the true qualities of patience and perseverance inherent in Capricorn can show through.

You have good administrative ability and are a capable worker, and if you are careful you can accumulate wealth. But you must be cautious and take professional advice in partnerships, as you are open to deception. You may be interested in social or welfare work, which suit your organisational skills and sympathy for others.

Moon in Aquarius

The Moon in Aquarius makes you an active and agreeable person with a friendly, easy-going nature. Sympathetic to the needs of others, you flourish in a laid-back atmosphere. You are broad-minded, fair and open to suggestion, although sometimes you have an unconventional quality which others can find hard to understand.

You are interested in the strange and curious, and in old articles and places. You enjoy trips to these places and gain much from them. Political, scientific and educational work interests you and you might choose a career in science or technology.

Money-wise, you make gains through innovation and concentration and Lunar Aquarians often tackle more than one job at a time. In love you are kind and honest.

Moon in Pisces

You have a kind, sympathetic nature, somewhat retiring at times, but you always take account of others' feelings and help when you can.

Personal relationships may be problematic, but as life goes on you can learn from your experiences and develop a better understanding of yourself and the world around you.

You have a fondness for travel, appreciate beauty and harmony and hate disorder and strife. You may be fond of literature and would make a good writer or speaker yourself. You have a creative imagination and may come across as an incurable romantic. You have strong intuition, maybe bordering on a mediumistic quality, which sets you apart from the mass. You may not be rich in cash terms, but your personal gifts are worth more than gold.

LEO IN LOVE

Discover how compatible in love you are with people from the same and other signs of the zodiac. Five stars equals a match made in heaven!

Leo meets Leo

More of a mutual appreciation society than a relationship, this is a promising match. Leo is kind, considerate, lofty, idealistic and brave, all qualities which are mirrored by a Leo partner. Both Lions will be determined in their ambitions, recognise the importance of the family and share a mutual love in all areas of their lives. Furthermore, Leo loves to be loved and so will give and receive it in equal amounts. There won't be many arguments but when there are – watch out! Star rating: *****

Leo meets Virgo

There is a chance for this couple, but it won't be trouble-free. Leo and Virgo view life very differently: Virgo is of a serious nature, struggling to relate to Leo's relentless optimism and cheerfulness, and even finding it annoying. Leo, meanwhile, may find Virgo stodgy, sometimes dark, and uninspiring. The saving grace comes through communication – Leo knows how to make Virgo talk, which is what it needs. If this pair find happiness, though, it may be a case of opposites attract! Star rating: ***

Leo meets Libra

The biggest drawback here is likely to be in the issue of commitment. Leo knows everything about constancy and faithfulness, a lesson which, sadly, Libra needs to learn. Librans are easy-going and diplomatic, qualities which are useful when Leo is on the war-path. This couple should be compatible on a personal level and any problems tend to relate to the different way in which these signs deal with outside factors. With good will and an open mind, it can work out well enough. Star rating: ***

Leo meets Scorpio

Stand back and watch the sparks fly! Scorpio has the deep sensitivity of a Water sign but it is also partially ruled by Fire planet Mars, from which it draws a great power that Leo will find difficult. Leo loves to take charge and really hates to feel psychologically undermined, which is Scorpio's stock-in-trade. Scorpio may find Leo's ideals a little shallow, which will be upsetting to the Lion. Anything is possible, but this possibility is rather slimmer than most. Star rating: **

Leo meets Sagittarius

An excellent match, as Leo and Sagittarius have so much in common. Their general approach to life is very similar, although as they are both Fire signs they can clash impressively! Sagittarius is shallower and more flippant than Leo likes to think of itself, and the Archer will be the one taking emotional chances. Sagittarius has met its match in the Lion's den, as brave Leo won't be outdone by anyone. Financially, they will either be very wealthy or struggling, and family life may be chaotic. Problems, like joys, are handled jointly – and that leads to happiness. Star rating: *****

Leo meets Capricorn

Despite promising appearances, this match often fails to thrive. Capricorn focuses on long-term objectives and, like Leo, is very practical. Both signs are capable of attaining success after a great struggle, which while requiring effort, gives them a mutual goal. But when life is easier, the cracks begin to show. Capricorn can be too serious for Leo, and the couple share few ideals. Leo loves luxury, Capricorn seeks austerity. Leo is warm but Capricorn seems cold and wintry in comparison. Both have many good points, but they don't seem to fire each other off properly. Star rating: **

Leo meets Aquarius

The problem here is that Aquarius doesn't 'think' in the general sense of the word, it 'knows'. Leo, on the other hand, is more practical and relies more on logical reasoning, and consequently it doesn't understand Aquarius very well. Aquarians can also appear slightly frosty in their appreciation of others and this, too, will eventually annoy Leo. This is a good match for a business partnership because Aquarius is astute, while Leo is brave, but personally the prognosis is less promising. Tolerance, understanding and forbearance are all needed to make this work. Star rating: **

Leo meets Pisces

Pisces always needs to understand others, which makes Leo feel warm and loved, while Leo sees, to its delight, that Pisces needs to be protected and taken care of. Pisceans are often lacking in self-confidence, which is something Leo has to spare, and happily it is often infectious. Pisces' inevitable cares are swept away on a tide of Leonine cheerfulness. This couple's home would be cheerful, and full of love which is beneficial to all family members. This is not a meeting of minds, but rather an understanding and appreciation of differences. Star rating: ****

Leo meets Aries

Stand by for action and make sure that the house is sound-proof! Leo is a lofty idealist and there is always likely to be friction when two Fire signs meet. To compensate, there is much mutual admiration, together with a desire to please. Where there are shared incentives, the prognosis is good but it's important not to let little irritations blow up. Both signs want to have their own way and this is a sure cause of trouble. There might not be much patience here, but there is plenty of action. Star rating: *****

Leo meets Taurus

Here we find a generally successful pairing, which frequently leads to an enduring relationship. Taurus needs stimulation which Leo is happy to offer, while Leo responds well to the Bull's sense of order. The essence of the relationship is balance, but it may be achieved with wild swings of the scales on the way, so don't expect a quiet life, though this pair will enjoy a reconciliation after an argument! Material success is probable and, as both like children, a family is likely. Star rating: ***

Leo meets Gemini

There can be problems here, but Gemini is adaptable enough to overcome many of them. Leo is a go-getter and might sometimes rail against Gemini's flighty tendencies, while Gemini's mental disorganisation can undermine Leo's practicality. However, Leo is cheerful and enjoys Gemini's jokey, flippant qualities. At times of personal intimacy, the two signs should be compatible. Leo and Gemini share very high ideals, but Leo will stick at them for longer. Patience is needed on both sides for the relationship to develop. Star rating: ***

Leo meets Cancer

This relationship will usually be directed by dominant Leo more towards its own needs than Cancer's. However, the Crab will willingly play second fiddle to more progressive and bossy types as it is deeply emotional and naturally supportive. Leo is bright, caring, magnanimous and protective and so, as long as it isn't over-assertive, this could be a good match. On the surface, Cancer appears the more conventional of the two, but Leo will discover, to its delight, that underneath it can be unusual and quirky. Star rating: ****

VENUS:
THE PLANET OF LOVE

If you look up at the sky around sunset or sunrise you will often see Venus in close attendance to the Sun. It is arguably one of the most beautiful sights of all and there is little wonder that historically it became associated with the goddess of love. But although Venus does play an important part in the way you view love and in the way others see you romantically, this is only one of the spheres of influence that it enjoys in your overall character.

Venus has a part to play in the more cultured side of your life and has much to do with your appreciation of art, literature, music and general creativity. Even the way you look is responsive to the part of the zodiac that Venus occupied at the start of your life, though this fact is also down to your Sun sign and Ascending sign. If, at the time you were born, Venus occupied one of the more gregarious zodiac signs, you will be more likely to wear your heart on your sleeve, as well as to be more attracted to entertainment, social gatherings and good company. If on the other hand Venus occupied a quiet zodiac sign at the time of your birth, you would tend to be more retiring and less willing to shine in public situations.

It's good to know what part the planet Venus plays in your life for it can have a great bearing on the way you appear to the rest of the world and since we all have to mix with others, you can learn to make the very best of what Venus has to offer you.

One of the great complications in the past has always been trying to establish exactly what zodiac position Venus enjoyed when you were born because the planet is notoriously difficult to track. However, we have solved that problem by creating a table that is exclusive to your Sun sign, which you will find on the following page.

Establishing your Venus sign could not be easier. Just look up the year of your birth on the following page and you will see a sign of the zodiac. This was the sign that Venus occupied in the period covered by your sign in that year. If Venus occupied more than one sign during the period, this is indicated by the date on which the sign changed, and the name of the new sign. For instance, if you were born in 1970, Venus was in Virgo until the 8th August, after which time it was in Libra. If you were born before 8th August your Venus sign is Virgo, if you were born on or after 8th August, your Venus sign is Libra. Once you have established the position of Venus at the time of your birth, you can then look in the pages which follow to see how this has a bearing on your life as a whole.

1911 VIRGO
1912 LEO / 13.8 VIRGO
1913 GEMINI / 6.8 CANCER
1914 VIRGO / 11.8 LIBRA
1915 CANCER / 4.8 LEO
1916 CANCER
1917 LEO / 28.7 VIRGO
1918 LEO / 25.7 VIRGO /
    19.8 LIBRA
1919 VIRGO
1920 LEO / 12.8 VIRGO
1921 GEMINI / 6.8 CANCER
1922 VIRGO / 11.8 LIBRA
1923 CANCER / 4.8 LEO
1924 GEMINI / 25.7 CANCER
1925 LEO / 28.7 VIRGO
1926 LEO / 24.7 VIRGO /
    18.8 LIBRA
1927 VIRGO
1928 LEO / 12.8 VIRGO
1929 GEMINI / 5.8 CANCER
1930 VIRGO / 10.8 LIBRA
1931 CANCER / 3.8 LEO
1932 GEMINI / 28.7 CANCER
1933 LEO / 27.7 VIRGO
1934 LEO / 23.7 VIRGO /
    17.8 LIBRA
1935 VIRGO
1936 LEO / 11.8 VIRGO
1937 GEMINI / 5.8 CANCER
1938 VIRGO / 10.8 LIBRA
1939 CANCER / 3.8 LEO
1940 GEMINI / 1.8 CANCER
1941 LEO / 27.7 VIRGO
1942 LEO / 23.7 VIRGO /
    17.8 LIBRA
1943 VIRGO
1944 LEO / 11.8 VIRGO
1945 GEMINI / 5.8 CANCER
1946 VIRGO / 9.8 LIBRA
1947 CANCER / 2.8 LEO
1948 GEMINI / 3.8 CANCER
1949 LEO / 26.7 VIRGO
1950 LEO / 23.7 VIRGO /
    16.8 LIBRA
1951 VIRGO
1952 LEO / 10.8 VIRGO
1953 GEMINI / 4.8 CANCER
1954 VIRGO / 9.8 LIBRA
1955 CANCER / 1.8 LEO
1956 GEMINI / 4.8 CANCER
1957 LEO / 26.7 VIRGO
1958 VIRGO / 16.8 LIBRA

1959 VIRGO
1960 LEO / 9.8 VIRGO
1961 GEMINI / 1.8 CANCER
1962 VIRGO / 9.8 LIBRA
1963 CANCER / 1.8 LEO
1964 GEMINI / 5.8 CANCER
1965 LEO / 25.7 VIRGO
1966 VIRGO / 16.8 LIBRA
1967 VIRGO
1968 LEO / 9.8 VIRGO
1969 GEMINI / 4.8 CANCER
1970 VIRGO / 8.8 LIBRA
1971 CANCER / 31.7 LEO
1972 GEMINI / 5.8 CANCER
1973 LEO / 25.7 VIRGO
1974 VIRGO / 15.8 LIBRA
1975 VIRGO
1976 LEO / 9.8 VIRGO
1977 GEMINI / 3.8 CANCER
1978 VIRGO / 8.8 LIBRA
1979 CANCER / 31.7 LEO
1980 GEMINI / 6.8 CANCER
1981 LEO / 24.7 VIRGO
1982 VIRGO / 15.8 LIBRA
1983 VIRGO
1984 LEO / 8.8 VIRGO
1985 GEMINI / 3.8 CANCER
1986 VIRGO / 7.8 LIBRA
1987 CANCER / 30.7 LEO
1988 GEMINI / 6.8 CANCER
1989 LEO / 24.7 VIRGO
1990 VIRGO / 14.8 LIBRA
1991 VIRGO / 22.8 LEO
1992 LEO / 8.8 VIRGO
1993 GEMINI / 2.8 CANCER
1994 VIRGO / 7.8 LIBRA
1995 CANCER / 30.7 LEO
1996 GEMINI / 7.8 CANCER
1997 LEO / 24.7 VIRGO
1998 VIRGO / 14.8 LIBRA
1999 VIRGO / 22.8 LEO
2000 LEO / 8.8 VIRGO
2001 GEMINI / 1.8 CANCER
2002 VIRGO / 8.8 LIBRA
2003 CANCER / 30.7 LEO
2004 GEMINI / 7.8 CANCER
2005 LEO / 24.7 VIRGO
2006 VIRGO / 14.8 LIBRA
2007 VIRGO / 22.8 LEO
2008 LEO / 8.8 VIRGO
2009 GEMINI / 1.8 CANCER

VENUS THROUGH THE ZODIAC SIGNS

Venus in Aries

Amongst other things, the position of Venus in Aries indicates a fondness for travel, music and all creative pursuits. Your nature tends to be affectionate and you would try not to create confusion or difficulty for others if it could be avoided. Many people with this planetary position have a great love of the theatre, and mental stimulation is of the greatest importance. Early romantic attachments are common with Venus in Aries, so it is very important to establish a genuine sense of romantic continuity. Early marriage is not recommended, especially if it is based on sympathy. You may give your heart a little too readily on occasions.

Venus in Taurus

You are capable of very deep feelings and your emotions tend to last for a very long time. This makes you a trusting partner and lover, whose constancy is second to none. In life you are precise and careful and always try to do things the right way. Although this means an ordered life, which you are comfortable with, it can also lead you to be rather too fussy for your own good. Despite your pleasant nature, you are very fixed in your opinions and quite able to speak your mind. Others are attracted to you and historical astrologers always quoted this position of Venus as being very fortunate in terms of marriage. However, if you find yourself involved in a failed relationship, it could take you a long time to trust again.

Venus in Gemini

As with all associations related to Gemini, you tend to be quite versatile, anxious for change and intelligent in your dealings with the world at large. You may gain money from more than one source but you are equally good at spending it. There is an inference here that you are a good communicator, via either the written or the spoken word, and you love to be in the company of interesting people. Always on the look-out for culture, you may also be very fond of music, and love to indulge the curious and cultured side of your nature. In romance you tend to have more than one relationship and could find yourself associated with someone who has previously been a friend or even a distant relative.

Venus in Cancer

You often stay close to home because you are very fond of family and enjoy many of your most treasured moments when you are with those you love. Being naturally sympathetic, you will always do anything you can to support those around you, even people you hardly know at all. This charitable side of your nature is your most noticeable trait and is one of the reasons why others are naturally so fond of you. Being receptive and in some cases even psychic, you can see through to the soul of most of those with whom you come into contact. You may not commence too many romantic attachments but when you do give your heart, it tends to be unconditionally.

Venus in Leo

It must become quickly obvious to almost anyone you meet that you are kind, sympathetic and yet determined enough to stand up for anyone or anything that is truly important to you. Bright and sunny, you warm the world with your natural enthusiasm and would rarely do anything to hurt those around you, or at least not intentionally. In romance you are ardent and sincere, though some may find your style just a little overpowering. Gains come through your contacts with other people and this could be especially true with regard to romance, for love and money often come hand in hand for those who were born with Venus in Leo. People claim to understand you, though you are more complex than you seem.

Venus in Virgo

Your nature could well be fairly quiet no matter what your Sun sign might be, though this fact often manifests itself as an inner peace and would not prevent you from being basically sociable. Some delays and even the odd disappointment in love cannot be ruled out with this planetary position, though it's a fact that you will usually find the happiness you look for in the end. Catapulting yourself into romantic entanglements that you know to be rather ill-advised is not sensible, and it would be better to wait before you committed yourself exclusively to any one person. It is the essence of your nature to serve the world at large and through doing so it is possible that you will attract money at some stage in your life.

Venus in Libra

Venus is very comfortable in Libra and bestows upon those people who have this planetary position a particular sort of kindness that is easy to recognise. This is a very good position for all sorts of friendships and also for romantic attachments that usually bring much joy into your life. Few individuals with Venus in Libra would avoid marriage and since you are capable of great depths of love, it is likely that you will find a contented personal life. You like to mix with people of integrity and intelligence but don't take kindly to scruffy surroundings or work that means getting your hands too dirty. Careful speculation, good business dealings and money through marriage all seem fairly likely.

Venus in Scorpio

You are quite open and tend to spend money quite freely, even on those occasions when you don't have very much. Although your intentions are always good, there are times when you get yourself in to the odd scrape and this can be particularly true when it comes to romance, which you may come to late or from a rather unexpected direction. Certainly you have the power to be happy and to make others contented on the way, but you find the odd stumbling block on your journey through life and it could seem that you have to work harder than those around you. As a result of this, you gain a much deeper understanding of the true value of personal happiness than many people ever do, and are likely to achieve true contentment in the end.

Venus in Sagittarius

You are lighthearted, cheerful and always able to see the funny side of any situation. These facts enhance your popularity, which is especially high with members of the opposite sex. You should never have to look too far to find romantic interest in your life, though it is just possible that you might be too willing to commit yourself before you are certain that the person in question is right for you. Part of the problem here extends to other areas of life too. The fact is that you like variety in everything and so can tire of situations that fail to offer it. All the same, if you choose wisely and learn to understand your restless side, then great happiness can be yours.

Venus in Capricorn

The most notable trait that comes from Venus in this position is that it makes you trustworthy and able to take on all sorts of responsibilities in life. People are instinctively fond of you and love you all the more because you are always ready to help those who are in any form of need. Social and business popularity can be yours and there is a magnetic quality to your nature that is particularly attractive in a romantic sense. Anyone who wants a partner for a lover, a spouse and a good friend too would almost certainly look in your direction. Constancy is the hallmark of your nature and unfaithfulness would go right against the grain. You might sometimes be a little too trusting.

Venus in Aquarius

This location of Venus offers a fondness for travel and a desire to try out something new at every possible opportunity. You are extremely easy to get along with and tend to have many friends from varied backgrounds, classes and inclinations. You like to live a distinct sort of life and gain a great deal from moving about, both in a career sense and with regard to your home. It is not out of the question that you could form a romantic attachment to someone who comes from far away or be attracted to a person of a distinctly artistic and original nature. What you cannot stand is jealousy, for you have friends of both sexes and would want to keep things that way.

Venus in Pisces

The first thing people tend to notice about you is your wonderful, warm smile. Being very charitable by nature you will do anything to help others, even if you don't know them well. Much of your life may be spent sorting out situations for other people, but it is very important to feel that you are living for yourself too. In the main, you remain cheerful, and tend to be quite attractive to members of the opposite sex. Where romantic attachments are concerned, you could be drawn to people who are significantly older or younger than yourself or to someone with a unique career or point of view. It might be best for you to avoid marrying whilst you are still very young.

LEO:
2008 DIARY PAGES

October

2008

1 WEDNESDAY ☿   *Moon Age Day 1   Moon Sign Libra*

You should have no problem getting on with others on this, the first day of October, though there may be occasions when you are tempted to bulldoze your ideas across to certain people. This is most likely with individuals who don't listen as carefully as you would wish. Patience is a virtue, though it may be lacking today.

2 THURSDAY ☿   *Moon Age Day 2   Moon Sign Scorpio*

You have scope to be at your best today when you are among close friends and people you trust a great deal. Be prepared to make a special fuss of your partner. Even though there may be no anniversary or special event to celebrate, sweeping someone off their feet can work wonders!

3 FRIDAY ☿   *Moon Age Day 3   Moon Sign Scorpio*

Household matters and issues from the past should take on a very pleasing aspect if you continue to stick to people you know well and to get the most from all domestic matters. You probably won't feel the need to push yourself unduly, and you can make much out of simply lazing around and making casual conversation with others.

4 SATURDAY ☿   *Moon Age Day 4   Moon Sign Sagittarius*

This can be a great time for creative self-expression. You can persuade others to value your opinions and to turn to you for the sort of advice you alone can offer. There is a strong recognition that you are somehow 'in the know', and even people living at a distance could be contacting you to pick your brains.

50

5 SUNDAY ☿ *Moon Age Day 5   Moon Sign Sagittarius*

Troublesome domestic matters are a possibility, but if you address these early in the day you will also leave yourself with sufficient time to please yourself later on. It's worth getting all necessary tasks out of the way well before the evening because this needs to be a time of freedom and personal choice for you.

6 MONDAY ☿ *Moon Age Day 6   Moon Sign Sagittarius*

Domestic issues are once again highlighted, and that might mean getting behind in other matters. Your best response is to exercise all the patience you can and simply do what seems most necessary. You can catch up later, and in any case it comes down to being a matter of priorities in the end.

7 TUESDAY ☿ *Moon Age Day 7   Moon Sign Capricorn*

The Moon's present position offers a temporary but nevertheless positive period for dealing well with all areas of your working life. You should have no problem whatsoever getting on with colleagues, and persuading them to be co-operative and to follow your lead. At home things should also be more settled.

8 WEDNESDAY ☿ *Moon Age Day 8   Moon Sign Capricorn*

Today and in fact all of the present period has potential to be easy-going and pleasantly enjoyable. With Venus now in your solar fourth house you can deal well with issues that arise in your personal life and should be on top of most of them before they become issues at all. Even generally tedious routines could seem pleasant now.

9 THURSDAY ☿ *Moon Age Day 9   Moon Sign Aquarius*

Communication issues could run into difficulty if you don't keep on top of them. The lunar low does little to help, and it is therefore very important that you double-check that messages are coming across as you intend. This is more likely to be an issue at work than in social settings.

10 FRIDAY ☿ *Moon Age Day 10   Moon Sign Aquarius*

The lunar low continues, potentially bringing a rather muddled feel to your thinking and actions. There is a funny side to this however, because others should find you charming and might be more than happy to smile kindly on your eccentricities.

11 SATURDAY ☿ *Moon Age Day 11   Moon Sign Aquarius*

Staying on top of things may not be at all easy, and you have to ask yourself whether it is even necessary in some cases. There might be certain issues that would be best left to their own devices, whilst you concentrate of matters that are self-evidently important. In any case your capabilities should be much improved tomorrow.

12 SUNDAY ☿ *Moon Age Day 12   Moon Sign Pisces*

A good deal of adapting will be necessary at the moment if you want to get the very best out of life. For the last few days you have been under the influence of a few slightly awkward planetary influences, and these could have left you feeling somewhat muddled. Today offers you the chance to think things through and to take action.

13 MONDAY ☿ *Moon Age Day 13   Moon Sign Pisces*

A restless streak starts to become evident, encouraging you to run a mile to avoid ordinary, everyday tasks. You might well need a change of scenery, and even if you only manage to get an hour or two in your local park it could be enough to make you feel entirely different. Learn to delegate and let others do some of the work.

14 TUESDAY ☿ *Moon Age Day 14   Moon Sign Aries*

Rather than being bossy at home, why not allow family members to choose options for themselves? Even if you don't mean to interfere, others may not be all that happy about the fact that you seem to know better than they do how to run their lives. If you listen and comment but avoid interference you can still have an input.

15 WEDNESDAY ☿   *Moon Age Day 15*   *Moon Sign Aries*

It might be better at the moment to consolidate certain areas of your life rather than setting out to change everything at the same time. Some of what you want to do is down to your own present restlessness, and for this reason alone you would be better off waiting for a while. A day to find something new and interesting to occupy your mind.

16 THURSDAY ☿   *Moon Age Day 16*   *Moon Sign Taurus*

Mercury remains in your solar third house, a sure sign that you can get most of your kicks at the moment from talking to and listening to those around you. There is good advice to be had, and some of it might come from rather unexpected directions. The more attention you pay, the greater is the chance you can benefit as a result.

17 FRIDAY   *Moon Age Day 17*   *Moon Sign Taurus*

This could be one of the best times of the month for involving yourself in community issues and for getting to grips with any problems that have a bearing on just about everyone you know. You can be very socially minded at the moment, and can allow the reforming tendencies of Leo to show out strongly. You might even be quite political.

18 SATURDAY   *Moon Age Day 18*   *Moon Sign Gemini*

In a family sense you should be able to find plenty to keep you occupied and full of beans this weekend. Although there may be chances to move about more, trends support activities close to home, and the greatest joys you encounter right now come courtesy of your more personal and domestic attachments.

19 SUNDAY   *Moon Age Day 19*   *Moon Sign Gemini*

Beware of allowing the views of others to influence your judgements to such an extent that you fail to address issues yourself. Leo might be just a little lazy at the moment, and for that reason alone it might be better simply to go with the flow. Don't be afraid to think about matters yourself and take whatever actions your mind suggests.

20 MONDAY
Moon Age Day 20   Moon Sign Cancer

A day to look for good moments in personal attachments and a definite increase in the power of love in your life. You have what it takes to make the most of your popularity, and also to pep up your social life. Constant attention from others can be wearing, but it can also feed your ego positively.

21 TUESDAY
Moon Age Day 21   Moon Sign Cancer

A few professional delays are a distinct possibility at the moment, and your best response to the situation is to wait and see. That might leave you with time on your hands, and since you can easily get restless right now you may decide to take on new projects that give your active mind something to think about.

22 WEDNESDAY
Moon Age Day 22   Moon Sign Leo

Stand by for an explosion of possibilities and do everything you can to meet this very progressive period in a reactive way. The lunar high should offer better general luck, together with a fund of new incentives and plenty of energy to pursue them. All in all this could be the most influential day that you will encounter during October.

23 THURSDAY
Moon Age Day 23   Moon Sign Leo

This is the best time of the month to be running ahead of the pack. If you use your quick thinking, some people may not be able to keep up with you. The new incentives continue and at the same time you have what it takes to sweep someone right off their feet. As a result, new romance is possible for some.

24 FRIDAY
Moon Age Day 24   Moon Sign Virgo

You need to keep moving and to follow up all possibilities as and when they arise. Even if there isn't too much time to spend with loved ones, a few words of reassurance might be all it takes to keep things sweet at home. Meanwhile you can afford to go wherever the action is and to stay well in charge of your own destiny.

25 SATURDAY   *Moon Age Day 25   Moon Sign Virgo*

Your sensitivity is heightened, enhancing your ability to support others today. One option is to find time to address issues that are associated with your home life, and family members should be pleased to have you around more. Your sunny and warm personality can be a joy to almost everyone you meet.

26 SUNDAY   *Moon Age Day 26   Moon Sign Virgo*

Home and family could well remain the most important consideration for you this Sunday, and even if friends urge you to do different things, many Leo subjects will be quite happy to stay around the homestead for the moment. New incentives come along tomorrow, but for the moment why not find a chair and sit in it?

27 MONDAY   *Moon Age Day 27   Moon Sign Libra*

Today's major trends are very different to the ones that had a bearing on you during the weekend. Now you may well feel quite charged and ready to look into the heart of any matter that has a part to play in your professional life. New responsibilities could be there for the taking, with offers that might seem very difficult to refuse.

28 TUESDAY   *Moon Age Day 28   Moon Sign Libra*

You can achieve a good balance of give and take right now, and can persuade certain individuals to be far more giving than might have been the case only a few days ago. With plenty of determination you shouldn't be easily beaten, though you may be forced to consider abandoning one particular issue.

29 WEDNESDAY   *Moon Age Day 0   Moon Sign Scorpio*

The present position of the Moon once again encourages you to turn your attention back to home and family. This is a reoccurring trend for you this month and the fact that you are so willing to work on behalf of those you love is not lost on the people in question. A great deal of genuine care and affection is now available to you.

30 THURSDAY
Moon Age Day 1   Moon Sign Scorpio

Organisational issues are to the fore at the moment. This could be related to work but is just as likely to be concerned with social issues, and there is scope for you to ring the changes in terms of out-of-work interests. An ideal day to think about people and places far away.

31 FRIDAY
Moon Age Day 2   Moon Sign Sagittarius

Don't be afraid to pursue romance and social pleasures with more abandon now. Even if others are inclined to be quieter and to take life more steadily now the autumn is firmly established, you have what it takes to push ahead with no thought of the changing weather or the darker nights. You relish life at present.

November
2008

1 SATURDAY
Moon Age Day 3   Moon Sign Sagittarius

Rather than allowing yourself to be manipulated by others, you would be wise to look at all situations yourself and to react according to your own conscience. Leo is a natural leader and not a follower, which is why in the end you can bring others round to your own point of view. It's a fine line though, because bullying won't work at present.

2 SUNDAY
Moon Age Day 4   Moon Sign Sagittarius

Life can be somewhat trying in some ways and yet very positive in others – it's simply a matter of choosing your path carefully for the moment. Even if you are on the receiving end of many social invitations, a part of your nature simply wants to force you ever closer to home, and the incentives to move around are not strong.

3 MONDAY
Moon Age Day 5   Moon Sign Capricorn

Your present ability to fully enjoy life could prove infectious to others, and you have scope to spread your goodwill far and wide today. Leo can be at its sunny and generous best, which means you can get everyone to love you. This is certainly a very positive way to begin a new week and a new month.

4 TUESDAY
Moon Age Day 6   Moon Sign Capricorn

For the professional types amongst you things might seem somewhat sluggish today and particularly by this afternoon. On the other hand, you can ensure there is enough happening in your personal and domestic scene to make you feel rather good about life generally. It's worth getting important jobs out of the way today if you can.

5 WEDNESDAY *Moon Age Day 7   Moon Sign Aquarius*

The lunar low has potential to take the wind out of your sails now, but perhaps not as much as would sometimes be the case. You can use the quieter tendencies that today brings in order to refuel your tanks and also for thinking ahead of yourself. Even if not everyone is on your side at the moment, you can bring them round when it matters.

6 THURSDAY *Moon Age Day 8   Moon Sign Aquarius*

Be prepared to keep life as simple as possible for the moment and not to complicate issues more than is necessary. An uncluttered day should leave you more time to think up future strategies, and to persuade colleagues and friends alike to be especially helpful. You can return the favours later.

7 FRIDAY *Moon Age Day 9   Moon Sign Aquarius*

Although you begin today with the Moon still occupying your opposite sign of Aquarius, this won't last long, and you can allow your confidence and social tendencies to grow as the day advances. Some sort of celebration might be in the offing to finish the day very well.

8 SATURDAY *Moon Age Day 10   Moon Sign Pisces*

Plenty of enjoyable things are possible as far as your social life is concerned, though personal attachments may need more attention on your part, and you could do worse than deliberately planning to sweep your partner or sweetheart off their feet in some way. Every little favour you do others today will be more than welcome.

9 SUNDAY *Moon Age Day 11   Moon Sign Pisces*

As the year gets older so you should be making a note of situations and belongings that you could quite happily do without. This is a time during which you have a chance to dump whatever is redundant, and with new possibilities coming your way all the time it could prove to be necessary. Beware of getting caught up in nostalgia right now.

10 MONDAY
Moon Age Day 12   Moon Sign Aries

If pleasure and enjoyment are high on your agenda now, you won't want to be so busy with practical issues that you fail to register the good times that are on offer. On the contrary, you now have what it takes to bring a great deal of joy to even the most mundane tasks, and on the way to put your entertaining side on display.

11 TUESDAY
Moon Age Day 13   Moon Sign Aries

Trends assist you to focus on the deeper aspects of your life at the moment, and to look very carefully not only at your actions but also at your motivations. This is fine as far as it goes, but you have to remember that you are a creature of the moment and that too much analysis can prove less than useful.

12 WEDNESDAY
Moon Age Day 14   Moon Sign Taurus

Though you are quite able to bring out the best in others in social situations right now, you may be having slightly less success making them keep their heads down at work. Part of the reason lies in the fact that you are so happy-go-lucky yourself at present. In addition, there are trends around indicating this to be a potentially positive time financially.

13 THURSDAY
Moon Age Day 15   Moon Sign Taurus

You have what it takes to attract a warm and positive response to your overtures from others around now, and you shouldn't have any difficulty at all pleasing the friends you already have and making a few more on the way. Attitude is very important when it comes to addressing superiors or people who can do you some good.

14 FRIDAY
Moon Age Day 16   Moon Sign Gemini

The Sun is presently in your solar fourth house, and can be extremely useful when it comes to your domestic life and the way you view family ties. If it now seems as though even usually awkward family members are behaving in an impeccable way, that offers you a chance to sort out home-based issues.

15 SATURDAY
Moon Age Day 17   Moon Sign Gemini

Your strong desire for social situations is noteworthy this weekend, and whether or not you work at the weekend you can afford to give your mind over to pleasure at some stage. If there are sufficient reasons to paint the town red you will be happy, but even if there are not you should be able to invent a few if you think long enough.

16 SUNDAY
Moon Age Day 18   Moon Sign Cancer

Stand by for a few challenges to your authority – or at least that is what it might look like from your point of view. As a Leo you are willing to give anyone a great deal of slack, but only up to a point. At base you do like to have your own way in the end, though prevailing planetary trends do little to assist you in this.

17 MONDAY
Moon Age Day 19   Moon Sign Cancer

A trip into the past might seem to be especially rewarding at the moment, and for once this could genuinely turn out to be the case for Leo. This is not because you are becoming especially nostalgic but rather because you are able to learn lessons as a result of happenings now long gone. It is upon such lessons that wisdom is founded.

18 TUESDAY
Moon Age Day 20   Moon Sign Leo

This has potential to be one of the best days of the month for getting what you want and for being able to keep everyone else happy on the way. You shouldn't be easily dissuaded from any course of action you want to take, but since you also have what it takes to talk others round to your particular point of view, you can make sure all is well.

19 WEDNESDAY
Moon Age Day 21   Moon Sign Leo

The positive interlude continues, offering you a chance to register a whole host of reasons why you can smile most of the time. Past successes become present ones, whilst you are also able to project yourself with great enthusiasm into situations that appear out of the blue. You can get life on your side now.

20 THURSDAY
Moon Age Day 22   Moon Sign Leo

For the third day in a row the Moon occupies your zodiac sign of Leo and from this position it continues to look favourably on your actions and your life generally. Family matters are particularly well enhanced at the moment, and your strength lies in the concern you show for the lives and motivations of younger people.

21 FRIDAY
Moon Age Day 23   Moon Sign Virgo

Even if you are still pushing forward very progressively, there are a few words of warning with regard to finances at the moment. You are not immune to a little bad luck when it comes to almost any sort of speculation, and losses are possible if you fail to think before you act. In almost every other respect you can keep life positive and happy.

22 SATURDAY
Moon Age Day 24   Moon Sign Virgo

This is a favourable moment for all interactive communications and for getting on well with anyone who sometimes causes you problems. Maybe their attitude has changed, but trends also assist you to bend your own nature to suit the situation. Look for the new and the unusual when it comes to social invitations.

23 SUNDAY
Moon Age Day 25   Moon Sign Libra

Most aspects of life can be aided now not by what you know but rather by who. Now is the time to keep your eye open for individuals who are in a position to help you out with an idea or a long-term plan for the future. It's worth finding time today to discuss such matters and to enlist the support of individuals you like and respect.

24 MONDAY
Moon Age Day 26   Moon Sign Libra

Romantic issues now have potential to be far more rewarding than may have seemed to be the case in the recent past. This might be partly because you are finding the necessary time to concentrate on personal matters, but also because you can take advantage of a planetary line-up that is favouring love.

25 TUESDAY
Moon Age Day 27   Moon Sign Scorpio

Beware of being waylaid by domestic chores or considerations at the moment, particularly if you are busy with the practical necessities of life. Don't be too quick to take offence when a colleague or friend seems to be critical. What they are saying may well be for your own good – even if that seems doubtful.

26 WEDNESDAY
Moon Age Day 28   Moon Sign Scorpio

With Mars now in your solar fifth house you can make the most of surprises and a tendency for you to be rather more impulsive than would normally be the case. You can also show the very courageous side of your Leo nature and make friends and admirers as a result. Leo can afford to be all smiles and sunshine at the moment.

27 THURSDAY
Moon Age Day 29   Moon Sign Scorpio

If you seek out some very enjoyable company today you should relish the cut and thrust of a busy and enjoyable time. Not everyone may want to join in the fun and games, and it may be necessary to ask a few pertinent questions if someone close to you is especially quiet. Try to draw them out and to discover what is wrong.

28 FRIDAY
Moon Age Day 0   Moon Sign Sagittarius

The Sun has now entered your solar fifth house, an influence that enhances all pleasure pursuits, pareticularly a tendency to shop until you drop. That's fine just as long as you are not spending money you don't really have. In any case some of the most enjoyable possibilities today needn't cost you a penny if you pay attention.

29 SATURDAY
Moon Age Day 1   Moon Sign Sagittarius

Another ideal day for making a splash socially, and for being extremely entertaining company when with your friends. Just about any sort of 'do' would probably suit you fine this weekend and especially so if you can put on your glad rags and appear at your brightest and most gregarious best.

30 SUNDAY   *Moon Age Day 2   Moon Sign Capricorn*

If the necessities of life appear to be limiting your personal freedom today, that may be only because you are holding onto issues that you could reasonably abandon right now. You may decide that a fresh approach to some aspects of your life is necessary, together with the input of your partner or some very close friends.

December

2008

1 MONDAY
Moon Age Day 3   Moon Sign Capricorn

Your love life and romantic matters are generally well starred, so you need to ensure that you are putting in sufficient effort. In a more mundane sense present planetary trends indicate that this would be just about the best time for getting others to back your ideas.

2 TUESDAY
Moon Age Day 4   Moon Sign Capricorn

Beware of taking too many risks today, especially later on. The Moon is moving rapidly towards Aquarius and that supports a slower period for a couple of days. This can at least offer scope for thought and allow you to step back from the rush and push that is indicated by other planetary trends at the moment.

3 WEDNESDAY
Moon Age Day 5   Moon Sign Aquarius

The lunar low this time around offers a chance for circumspection and for looking back, rather than projecting your ideas into the future. It shouldn't be too much of a struggle to force yourself to take time out to do whatever takes your fancy. In any case trying too hard today and tomorrow probably won't work.

4 THURSDAY
Moon Age Day 6   Moon Sign Aquarius

If energy and enthusiasm remain in generally short supply for now, the best way you can enjoy today is to let others do most of the work whilst you sit back and supervise. Leo can be quite good at delegating, and in any case the time is probably right to let others, and especially younger people, have their moment.

5 FRIDAY
Moon Age Day 7   Moon Sign Pisces

When it comes to getting on with things you could now discover that working in pairs can work wonders. Trends encourage a natural tendency to group together with like-minded individuals and to seek out help when you need it the most. Your naturally warm and happy disposition can begin to show through again.

6 SATURDAY
Moon Age Day 8   Moon Sign Pisces

A more hectic period is indicated when it comes to the social and romantic side of your life, and this could not come at a better time than on a Saturday. For some Leos the round of gatherings and parties might already be underway, and you can put yourself in the right frame of mind to get the very best from anything that is on offer.

7 SUNDAY
Moon Age Day 9   Moon Sign Pisces

Why not get out and about today? It doesn't really matter where because the important factor is the new input you can gain as a result. Humdrum and everyday jobs are what you will be seeking to avoid – either leaving them to others or ignoring them altogether. Life itself can be your best teacher at present, as you are about to discover.

8 MONDAY
Moon Age Day 10   Moon Sign Aries

Personal relationships can be much enhanced this week by the position of Venus, which has now moved into the seventh house of your solar chart. Your natural sensitivity to others is well marked and you have what it takes to make the best of impressions – even on people who don't normally find you attractive.

9 TUESDAY
Moon Age Day 11   Moon Sign Aries

It is very important for you today to spare more than a passing thought for the feelings and sensibilities of your partner. If you are not involved in one specific relationship at present the trends are still around, but they will have a bearing on close family ties. Be prepared to take time out to work out why others are behaving in the way they are.

10 WEDNESDAY   *Moon Age Day 12   Moon Sign Taurus*

There are signs that you could fall foul of a few practical problems today, particularly if you are tending to rush things too much. Slow down and think things through before you get carried away. Also make sure that really necessary jobs are out of the way before you turn to having fun.

11 THURSDAY   *Moon Age Day 13   Moon Sign Taurus*

A period of enjoyment and emotional fulfilment is on offer, though once again it is important that you take note of what is happening around you if you want to get the very best from these trends. One thing is more or less certain – you have scope to get more of your own way now without having to work too hard to do so.

12 FRIDAY   *Moon Age Day 14   Moon Sign Gemini*

Even if you are very much wrapped up in yourself and your own needs just now, there could be an increasing tendency for you to be turning your mind outwards, towards those individuals who you sense have had a really rough deal from life. Maybe it's the time of year, but you can afford to show your charitable side.

13 SATURDAY   *Moon Age Day 15   Moon Sign Gemini*

Getting yourself into the limelight shouldn't be difficult this weekend, and the approach of the festive season offers activities that should turn out to be a great deal of fun. Whether you are with friends, colleagues or your partner, now is the time to shake free from the bounds of convention and to do something extraordinary!

14 SUNDAY   *Moon Age Day 16   Moon Sign Cancer*

Like yesterday, you now have what it takes to adopt any kind of prominent role and to put yourself at the centre of whatever is taking place in your vicinity. This is Leo at its best, and you shouldn't be stuck for ideas, even when others are finding the going difficult. If there is any race to win, Leo can make the tape first.

15 MONDAY   *Moon Age Day 17   Moon Sign Cancer*

By tomorrow the trends are more positive, but today should at least offer you the chance to pause and think. If December has been particularly busy as far as you are concerned, there is nothing at all wrong with having the odd day to sit back and take stock of all that is happening.

16 TUESDAY   *Moon Age Day 18   Moon Sign Leo*

The focus is on Lady Luck, even if you don't realise the fact until sometime further down the line. Make this a day to remember by taking command of situations and by refusing to take no for an answer when you feel a yes in your soul. Leo is now potentially aspiring, noble, courageous and determined. Wow! What a person you can be.

17 WEDNESDAY   *Moon Age Day 19   Moon Sign Leo*

Major endeavours and undertakings go better when you are involved, and you can persuade others of this fact. This is not a time during which you will have to fight to be heard. On the contrary, your positive attitude to life should be appealing to others. Why not show your romantic side today?

18 THURSDAY   *Moon Age Day 20   Moon Sign Virgo*

You can now take advantage of a phase of definite harmony in personal and romantic attachments. Working together as one of a pair should seem quite natural to you, and even where there has been disagreement and disharmony, you can now ensure that peace prevails. Give some extra thought to those last-minute presents.

19 FRIDAY   *Moon Age Day 21   Moon Sign Virgo*

In terms of your financial life there are signs that you may have to alter your planning in some way. Maybe an investment you made is ceasing to give the return you would wish, or it could be that you decide to rethink your overall strategies. There is time today to consider such matters, and incentives to do so.

20 SATURDAY
Moon Age Day 22   Moon Sign Libra

A boost to your powers of communication is available as the Moon enters your solar third house. Other trends add to this and may offer a chance for you to reach a definite realisation regarding something that has been hidden to you previously. Even if today is weird in some ways, it is also fascinating.

21 SUNDAY
Moon Age Day 23   Moon Sign Libra

Expressing yourself in gatherings of people may not be easy today, but the same will not be true in an intimate sense. You know exactly the right words to say in order to make someone feel really good, and if you are specifically looking at the possibility of making a romantic conquest, do it today!

22 MONDAY
Moon Age Day 24   Moon Sign Scorpio

All matters to do with house and home are well accented and the position of the Moon assists you to draw closer and closer to loved ones. Your strength lies in recognising the needs that others have of you and being selfless in your approach to most situations. It looks as though the Lion has taken on a good dose of Christmas spirit.

23 TUESDAY
Moon Age Day 25   Moon Sign Scorpio

You have scope to bring a practical plan to fruition very nicely, and you shouldn't have to look too far to find the answers you require. If you seek out help from friends and colleagues alike, it is possible that you can put something important to bed ahead of the prolonged period of festivities that lie ahead of you.

24 WEDNESDAY
Moon Age Day 26   Moon Sign Scorpio

When it comes to romance especially you need to be in charge, and you may not take very kindly if others are manipulating you in some way. You can afford to forget such matters and concentrate on wrapping those last-minute presents instead. It soon won't matter who is steering the ship of romance – just enjoy the voyage!

25 THURSDAY   *Moon Age Day 27   Moon Sign Sagittarius*

Special attachments allow you to put a big smile on your face for Christmas Day, and everything comes together in a planetary sense to offer you the best of times. Not everyone will enjoy themselves of course, but that's Christmas. Be prepared to leave the miseries alone and concentrate on the fun types.

26 FRIDAY   *Moon Age Day 28   Moon Sign Sagittarius*

As with yesterday, you can achieve some very happy moments in terms of romantic attachments, though you may also be slightly more restless for Boxing Day and keen to get away from the remnants of the turkey. An ideal day to descend on a good friend who will be relieved to see you.

27 SATURDAY   *Moon Age Day 0   Moon Sign Capricorn*

Your personal ego is very strong at the moment and you could so easily lose your temper if others cross you about issues that you see as being your own. Rather than flying off the handle, it's worth remembering the time of year and letting things flow over you. Routines have a part to play in today's proceedings.

28 SUNDAY   *Moon Age Day 1   Moon Sign Capricorn*

Venus remains in your solar seventh house, which continues to be especially good in terms of personal attachments. In a more practical sense it is important to realise that all that glistens is not gold. Bear in mind that today is not ideal for large financial investments or for signing any sort of document.

29 MONDAY   *Moon Age Day 2   Moon Sign Capricorn*

The Sun is now occupying your solar sixth house, a highly favourable position that will, in the New Year, assist you to master new skills and do very well at work. For the moment it could bring the odd frustration, because for many Lions the presence of Christmas means not being able to get on with things in the way they would wish.

30 TUESDAY   *Moon Age Day 3   Moon Sign Aquarius*

The lunar low this month coincides with the end of the year, so you may not be in the mood to continue to push the boat out in terms of celebrations. Chances are you are already straining at the leash to do something more practical, because even the fun-loving Lion can only take so many party games. Keep a sense of proportion today.

31 WEDNESDAY   *Moon Age Day 4   Moon Sign Aquarius*

The very best New Year celebrations are possible if you put yourself in the company of people you know well and who you love to have around. Huge gatherings might not appeal whilst the lunar low is around, but there are sufficient good planetary influences to support a good time and a sense of fun.

LEO:
2009 DIARY PAGES

LEO:
2009 IN BRIEF

There are times at the start of this year when you have to be a little careful about what you are taking on. This is not because you will come unstuck but merely because you expect too much of yourself. January and February offer many incentives, and your working life especially should be looking good. Don't let people bog you down with details because it is the overall picture that matters the most. Keep up your efforts to involve new people in some of your schemes.

March and April should find you moving forward on most fronts. Extra care will be necessary in relationships, mainly because of possible misunderstandings. Keep in touch with friends at a distance and don't turn down the chance of making a move at work, even if this means a total reorganisation. On the social front you seem to be enjoying a varied time and will be getting to know some new and significant people.

May and June bring the start of the summer and a chance for Leo to really start moving. It is during the warmer months that you generally do best and at this time you should be filled with boundless energy. You may have to be careful not to upset colleagues or friends during June, and it would be sensible for you to check and double-check details before embarking on long-distance travel.

Give yourself extra credit for your successes in July and August. There will be more to shout about in financial terms and you will also be right on the ball when it comes to thinking up new strategies. If not everyone is on your side, talk them round because that's a skill you possess in great measure at this time. Personalities of one sort or another could be entering your life and you could achieve a little success by implication. Socially speaking you are definitely a star.

With the autumn you may have to stop and retrench a little. The fact is that you have gone as far as you can in a particular direction and now you need to start something new. September and October give you every chance to reorder and to be as progressive as you would wish to be. This is one of the best periods of the entire year for love and for making the best of impressions on almost everyone. Some unexpected travel may become possible towards the end of October.

November and December will go by in a flash. You will be so busy and so committed to what you are doing that there will be hardly a moment to spare. You can count on being generally happy with your lot and can also rely a good deal on the support that comes from family and friends.

January
2009

1 THURSDAY
Moon Age Day 5   Moon Sign Aquarius

The year starts in a positive way for you if you capitalise on the good and useful ideas that are coming into your head. Even if it isn't possible to put many of these into action for the moment, you can at least be ingenious and clever. Any limitations around now are linked to the position of the Moon.

2 FRIDAY
Moon Age Day 6   Moon Sign Pisces

The present position of the Sun in your solar chart assists you to get moving very rapidly in directions that will be of tremendous use to you during January. There is no time to waste, and that is why you might get slightly frustrated if you are still being slowed down by the end of the Christmas and New Year holidays.

3 SATURDAY
Moon Age Day 7   Moon Sign Pisces

From an emotional point of view you can afford to be very supportive today and to find time to offer a helping hand to both friends and family members, who should relish your company and advice. On the romantic front you now have what it takes to pick up the pace in relationships.

4 SUNDAY
Moon Age Day 8   Moon Sign Aries

There could be extra work about today, and this may surprise you on a Sunday. Even if you don't have a great deal of time to spend on yourself, you can at least dedicate your efforts to the happiness of those around you. Look out for a slight upward trend in finances, perhaps brought about by your own actions.

5 MONDAY
Moon Age Day 9   Moon Sign Aries

Your imagination is definitely enhanced by present astrological trends, enabling you to approach new situations with a real expectation that you are going to succeed. Your best response to any negative vibes, particularly at work, is to fend them off as best you can and stay positive.

6 TUESDAY
Moon Age Day 10   Moon Sign Taurus

There should be time enough today to attend to everything you see as being important in a professional and practical sense, whilst at the same time having moments to spare that you can lavish on loved ones. Be prepared to help out anyone who needs advice, even if you have little experience in what ails them.

7 WEDNESDAY
Moon Age Day 11   Moon Sign Taurus

It is the very practical qualities of your nature that count today, and you can afford to pitch into anything new with a sure and certain knowledge that you can cope well enough. This is laudable, though there may be times when it would be wise to seek the advice and assistance of someone who is a genuine expert.

8 THURSDAY
Moon Age Day 12   Moon Sign Gemini

As the Moon moves on in your solar chart so it assists you to be more communicative, less inclined to hold to your own views and very much more co-operative. This has to be a good thing because the Lion in isolation is not a happy creature. You have much to contribute with your common sense and good humour.

9 FRIDAY
Moon Age Day 13   Moon Sign Gemini

You needn't hold back if people genuinely want to know what you think. You won't have to worry too much about being diplomatic, particularly if that comes quite naturally to you at this stage of the month. The spotlight is on romance, and if you have been looking for a new love this is the right time to concentrate your efforts.

10 SATURDAY   *Moon Age Day 14   Moon Sign Cancer*

Now that the Moon in entering your solar twelfth house you can take advantage of a couple of slightly quieter days. Trends encourage you to be more thoughtful and less inclined to offer an opinion unless you are asked directly. None of this need prevent you from making practical progress, even if it is fairly low-key.

11 SUNDAY   *Moon Age Day 15   Moon Sign Cancer*

There is definitely room for thoughtfulness and quiet moments on this particular Sunday. Although you can afford to be friendly, there may be a part of your nature that simply wants to contemplate. This trend is very short-lived because by tomorrow you can get everything working to your positive advantage again.

12 MONDAY   ☿   *Moon Age Day 16   Moon Sign Leo*

Today marks the start of the lunar high – that part of each month when the Moon returns to your own zodiac sign of Leo. You have scope to be fired up with energy, keen to get on with things and much luckier than of late. Taking silly chances wouldn't be wise, though the odd speculation could pay off at this time.

13 TUESDAY   ☿   *Moon Age Day 17   Moon Sign Leo*

Now there is everything to play for, particularly if you are more competitive and less inclined to hold back. At work it's time to be quite bold and more than willing to offer your point of view. For some Leo subjects advancement could be available – though not without some effort on your part.

14 WEDNESDAY ☿   *Moon Age Day 18   Moon Sign Virgo*

You can't expect to get on with everyone, and it is possible today that one or two people could prove to be very difficult to deal with. If this turns out to be the case your best approach is to avoid them altogether, in favour of individuals who give you no problems. Don't try too hard to change the world today – just live in it!

15 THURSDAY ☿ *Moon Age Day 19 Moon Sign Virgo*

Once you have made up your mind to a particular course of action now, you needn't let anything prevent you from getting your own way. You can be quite stubborn when necessary, but you also have what it takes to increase your popularity with colleagues and superiors alike. It's worth saving time for family later on.

16 FRIDAY ☿ *Moon Age Day 20 Moon Sign Libra*

It is the strange nuances of life that have potential to captivate your imagination today. You could be subject to all sorts of bizarre coincidences or little happenings that you can't properly explain. Take note of these with a view to turning particular situations to your distinct advantage later.

17 SATURDAY ☿ *Moon Age Day 21 Moon Sign Libra*

Beware of being too quick to take offence today, because not all the remarks made by others are directed at you. There is plenty of opportunity this weekend to shine in a social sense, especially if you are willing to co-operate and become one of a team. If affairs of the heart are proving slightly problematical, be prepared to tread carefully.

18 SUNDAY ☿ *Moon Age Day 22 Moon Sign Libra*

An ideal day for some sort of outing, and for capitalising on any good deals that are on offer. With everything to play for in terms of money matters, trends assist you to strengthen your financial position, and to make the most of opportunities, perhaps even in terms of some unexpected cash.

19 MONDAY ☿ *Moon Age Day 23 Moon Sign Scorpio*

The time is right to keep up the pressure at work and show what you are made of by thinking for yourself at all times. Your sunny disposition can be a positive joy amidst the winter weather, representing a breath of summer on cold days. When it comes to thinking up the right thing to say at the best time, you are second to none now.

20 TUESDAY ☿ *Moon Age Day 24 Moon Sign Scorpio*

You may not take too kindly to being given instructions at the moment, especially if the person handing them out has no real idea what they are talking about. There is a limit to your patience when you are dealing with those you see as idiots, but there are times when it would be better to count to ten than to lose your temper.

21 WEDNESDAY ☿ *Moon Age Day 25 Moon Sign Sagittarius*

Current influences suggest slightly slower reactions than usual, and the possibility of minor irritations and irrational mishaps. You can best circumnavigate these trends by concentrating more and by only taking on one job at once. You may not take kindly to people who think they know how you should live your life better than you do.

22 THURSDAY ☿ *Moon Age Day 26 Moon Sign Sagittarius*

Personality clashes are a risk today, particularly if you are coming up against people who can be as stubborn as you. When an irresistible force meets an immovable object, something has to give – and it might have to be you. Avoid blank refusals if invitations come along, because you can benefit from the change.

23 FRIDAY ☿ *Moon Age Day 27 Moon Sign Sagittarius*

Once again the focus is on money and the ways you can get more of it. If you like to live a fairly luxurious life when it proves to be possible, you can probably sometimes spend fairly lavishly. However, your shrewdness is well starred at the moment, assisting you to find ways of getting good value for money.

24 SATURDAY ☿ *Moon Age Day 28 Moon Sign Capricorn*

The weekend offers a break from routines and a time when you can pause for thought. Rather than staying locked up in the house, why not get wrapped up and take yourself off into the fresh air? You have what it takes to persuade others to go along with you, and can capitalise on the positive social trends today and tomorrow.

25 SUNDAY ☿ *Moon Age Day 29   Moon Sign Capricorn*

Now is the time to think on your feet. Not all the answers you require will be around you all the time, and it's worth bringing your strong intuition into play. Speaking of playing, your fun side is now highlighted, as are certain competitive traits. If you really do want to win, there are gains to be made by trying hard today.

26 MONDAY ☿ *Moon Age Day 0   Moon Sign Aquarius*

The start of a new week coincides with the lunar low – that period that comes along each month when the Moon enters your opposite zodiac sign. You can take advantage of this period by remaining fairly subdued and by watching what is happening around you. Too much effort at this time might be entirely wasted.

27 TUESDAY ☿ *Moon Age Day 1   Moon Sign Aquarius*

Be prepared to listen and watch, and only react when you know the time is right. You can afford to let others take some of the strain at the present time, whilst you recharge flagging batteries. Nobody can keep up a frenetic pace indefinitely, and it won't do you any harm at all to spend a few hours planning rather than doing.

28 WEDNESDAY ☿ *Moon Age Day 2   Moon Sign Aquarius*

Even if your responses are slow at first today, as the hours pass you can begin to get back to normal. By the evening you could be full of beans again and quite anxious to do something different. A certain amount of restlessness is indicated, and you can best deal with this by turning your active mind in new and alternative directions.

29 THURSDAY ☿ *Moon Age Day 3   Moon Sign Pisces*

This may be the best time of the month to get new schemes up and running. You have had plenty of time to plan your strategies, so now you can come out fighting. Of course there could be occasions when you will defend yourself before you are attacked, but your strength lies in realising when you've made a mistake.

78

30 FRIDAY   ☿   *Moon Age Day 4   Moon Sign Pisces*

Your sunny and warm nature reflects the Sun, which is your ruling planet. It will be the high summer before you are really at your fantastic best, but for now your best approach is to encourage and push forward in a fairly slow and steady way. Trends support a focus on your family and your life partner.

31 SATURDAY   ☿   *Moon Age Day 5   Moon Sign Aries*

You can continue to be a positive inspiration to practically everyone who has a part to play in your day, and to give more to life than you take from it. This weekend has much to offer in terms of social happenings, and instead of just being the life and soul of any party, it may well be you who is organising most of them!

February

2009

1 SUNDAY
Moon Age Day 6   Moon Sign Aries

The first day of February offers a chance to go with the plans of family members or friends, but without getting involved in disputes or arguments that break out in the family. You may decide to withdraw from situations of confrontation – if only because you can be so forceful when you do get involved.

2 MONDAY
Moon Age Day 7   Moon Sign Taurus

The opportunities for professional gains should now be considerable. You are at the start of a high-profile period during which you can show your Leo nature to its best advantage. Steam ahead towards success and ask others to help you out if you need to. You needn't let any minor aches and pains hamper progress.

3 TUESDAY
Moon Age Day 8   Moon Sign Taurus

Twosomes are well accented for you right now. The focus is on co-operating in some way, whether this is in business or in your personal life. The time is right to share as much as you can, and to make the adage 'two heads are better than one' work to your advantage at every opportunity.

4 WEDNESDAY
Moon Age Day 9   Moon Sign Taurus

Small tensions between yourself and your life partner are possible now that Mars is in your solar seventh house. You needn't allow this to cast a cloud over your life, although a little extra attention to their needs and wants might be sensible. Even if it seems a long way to a specific destination, you might be there before you know it.

5 THURSDAY
Moon Age Day 10   Moon Sign Gemini

Unexpected and quite interesting communications can offer new opportunities, and you can capitalise on surprises in different areas of your life. This would be a great time for making a spontaneous trip with your partner or a friend, and even if you have to travel on business you could discover a lot of interesting facts on the way.

6 FRIDAY
Moon Age Day 11   Moon Sign Gemini

If you now decide that you are not getting where you want to be in terms of your professional life, it's worth considering some fairly radical changes in the not too distant future. Getting your head round the motivations of those you are close to might be rather more difficult today than it is normally.

7 SATURDAY
Moon Age Day 12   Moon Sign Cancer

The Moon moves into your solar twelfth house today, offering a couple of slightly quieter days. This need not necessarily be a bad thing, particularly if you use the time to consider certain matters more deeply and to get on with things at your own pace. Love should be as strong as ever at present.

8 SUNDAY
Moon Age Day 13   Moon Sign Cancer

Many Leos can make the most of a steady and even a dreamy sort of day, and one on which you needn't be forced to do anything that goes against the grain. With a chance to catch up on your own thoughts and with the promise of a very positive phase in front of you, you have definite scope to clear the decks for action.

9 MONDAY
Moon Age Day 14   Moon Sign Leo

The Moon now races into your zodiac sign of Leo, so it's time for the action to begin! A new week offers the chance of new starts for you, and operating at lightning speed is the order of the day. Make the most of your energy today, even if others find it very difficult to keep up with your frenetic pace.

10 TUESDAY
Moon Age Day 15   Moon Sign Leo

Be prepared to take the initiative where plans and schemes are concerned, rather than leaving them to the caprices of other people. The rest of the world won't necessarily have your energy or know-how, and it is vitally important today that you feel yourself to be in command. An ideal day to contact people you don't see very often.

11 WEDNESDAY
Moon Age Day 16   Moon Sign Virgo

With the Sun now in your seventh house you can ensure this is a far easier and more straightforward period in terms of personal attachments than is sometimes the case for the Lion. This can act as a boost to your love life and assist you to express your emotions. Your strength now lies in leaving the past far behind.

12 THURSDAY
Moon Age Day 17   Moon Sign Virgo

Trends support a great deal of versatility at the moment, and you can put this to good use in any number of ways. Even if others find life and situations to be complicated, you have what it takes to steam ahead and sort out problems as and when they occur. In affairs of the heart, a little more originality may be called for.

13 FRIDAY
Moon Age Day 18   Moon Sign Libra

OK, so it's Friday the thirteenth, but that needn't mean bad luck as far as you are concerned. On the contrary, you can turn this into a fairly successful day and one on which you can make definite headway in terms of your wishes and desires. If other people are treading carefully, why not dash in and make gains?

14 SATURDAY
Moon Age Day 19   Moon Sign Libra

Now is the time to seek out others in your desire for greater excitement. It's worth identifying those with a great sense of adventure and a desire to break the bounds of the possible. Allied to such individuals you can become more daring, and might even surprise yourself with your courage and dexterity.

15 SUNDAY   *Moon Age Day 20   Moon Sign Scorpio*

It's time to assume a starring role. The Moon is in your solar fifth house and your persuasive talents are emphasised. If there is something you really want, this is the best day possible to ask for it. If you use your winning ways you can persuade those who care for you to agree to what to them will seem like reasonable requests.

16 MONDAY   *Moon Age Day 21   Moon Sign Scorpio*

Mercury now enhances your natural talent for communication, allied to your usual winning ways. There may be times at the moment when you have to stop what you are doing and start again from the beginning. Even if this is frustrating, your best response is to remain generally cheerful throughout.

17 TUESDAY   *Moon Age Day 22   Moon Sign Scorpio*

Try not to let anyone dominate your thoughts or actions at this time – not even your life partner. You really do know best what is right for you, and while tact is important with those who only have your best interests at heart, you might also need to be quite determined. It would be far too easy today to simply capitulate.

18 WEDNESDAY   *Moon Age Day 23   Moon Sign Sagittarius*

Personal attachments continue to have a generally co-operative element, but it's possible that you still feel as if your life isn't entirely your own. There are ways and means of dealing with this, but none of them involve you losing your temper. On the contrary, the more pleasant you are, the better all round.

19 THURSDAY   *Moon Age Day 24   Moon Sign Sagittarius*

You can now put the force of your personality to good use, and can achieve singular objectives by being your usual determined self. Fresh achievements are possible, with education and legacies being particularly well starred. You should also look for opportunities to use your present ingenuity to the full.

20 FRIDAY   *Moon Age Day 25   Moon Sign Capricorn*

The focus is now on the obligations you feel towards others, and you need to be careful that you don't bog yourself down with a sense of duty. Your best approach is to lighten the load whenever you can by going for excitement and something different. Nature itself has some messages for you at present.

21 SATURDAY   *Moon Age Day 26   Moon Sign Capricorn*

Trends encourage an exchange of ideas, though you may be reluctant to admit that others are right and you are quite definitely wrong. There is an element of stubbornness here, because there will always be occasions when you can learn from your mistakes. But you can't do so unless you are willing to admit they exist.

22 SUNDAY   *Moon Age Day 27   Moon Sign Capricorn*

By all means keep up the pace as Sunday comes along, but make sure that whatever you are doing is enjoyable. Never mind useful or strictly necessary for the moment. There are times when it is important to have some fun, and today is such a time for you. There's a chance to slow down markedly as the evening approaches.

23 MONDAY   *Moon Age Day 28   Moon Sign Aquarius*

This probably isn't going to be the most dynamic start to a new week that you have ever experienced. The lunar low supports a rather sluggish approach, and does little to help you to push yourself forward. On the contrary, it's worth withdrawing into yourself much more than usual, though this is a temporary phase.

24 TUESDAY   *Moon Age Day 29   Moon Sign Aquarius*

Things might appear to become unstable and certain plans are likely to become unworkable at this time. Instead of throwing in the towel and abandoning them altogether, why not watch and wait for a while? It won't be more than a few hours before you can get yourself back on form and moving forward again.

25 WEDNESDAY   *Moon Age Day 0   Moon Sign Pisces*

Any matter between yourself and your partner today can turn rather difficult unless you give it your full attention. It could be that someone is worrying much more than you are about a situation you see as being of little significance. However, if they are ill at ease, you would be wise to deal with the situation as soon as possible.

26 THURSDAY   *Moon Age Day 1   Moon Sign Pisces*

You can now be a very stimulating person to be with, and can sprinkle practically everything you do with magic. You can afford to approach situations with optimism and to show your warm personality all the time. Most important of all is your ability to show your concern for others in very tangible and practical ways.

27 FRIDAY   *Moon Age Day 2   Moon Sign Aries*

A phase of possible personal growth is on offer, and there is no end to what you can learn at the moment, purely by keeping your ears and eyes open. With plenty to set you apart from the herd, you have what it takes to make friends and to remain quite definite in your opinions. Don't be afraid to let people hear what you have to say.

28 SATURDAY   *Moon Age Day 3   Moon Sign Aries*

Meeting people, travelling and learning from your experiences are all favoured on this particular weekend. What matters the most is broadening your horizons, and this is something you achieve without really having to try. When you do put your mind to something, just imagine what you could achieve then.

March

2009

1 SUNDAY
Moon Age Day 4   Moon Sign Aries

If you are now in the middle of personal changes, it's worth considering whether there is a certain amount of baggage you have been carrying around that needs to be jettisoned. Although you may be happy with your lot in a personal sense, there may be room for improvement in certain practical aspects to your life.

2 MONDAY
Moon Age Day 5   Moon Sign Taurus

Try to engage in projects that need to be finished so that you will be in a position to take on new ones. If you complicate situations too much at the moment, you may get bogged down, and success will be harder to achieve. Affairs of the heart are well accented, and you can use this interlude to seek out new attachments.

3 TUESDAY
Moon Age Day 6   Moon Sign Taurus

Social arrangements may now have to be rerouted, and you need to be able to think on your feet if you are to avoid a fairly complicated sort of day. Don't be afraid of giving of your best at work, despite any possible problems coming from the direction of colleagues. Maybe they don't fully understand what you are trying to tell them.

4 WEDNESDAY
Moon Age Day 7   Moon Sign Gemini

Your social life and group ventures count for a great deal now, though there could be slightly less of a sense of satisfaction regarding family-based matters. It could be that you are failing to understand what it is that others really want of you. The problem is compounded if you sense that they don't really know either!

5 THURSDAY
Moon Age Day 8   Moon Sign Gemini

Trends indicate an impressionable Leo at this stage of the week, and the possibility of a bruised ego if you take offhand remarks too literally. This isn't a good reflection of your general nature, but if you are rather more sensitive than usual under present astrological influences, you would be wise to shield your ego somewhat.

6 FRIDAY
Moon Age Day 9   Moon Sign Cancer

A break with the past may prove to be a good thing around now. At the same time you may be noticing for the first time this year that the weather is changing and that spring is on the way. Both for today and across the weekend, there is much to be said for fresh air and the chance to fill your lungs in places you see as being beautiful.

7 SATURDAY
Moon Age Day 10   Moon Sign Cancer

Communication is highlighted in your life across this weekend, offering you the chance to get your message across to others in a very positive way. You may not have to plan everything in a moment-by-moment sense, and in fact can make plenty of progress if you simply react to situations that are taking place around you.

8 SUNDAY
Moon Age Day 11   Moon Sign Leo

The Moon returns to your zodiac sign and brings a Sunday on which you can make things work out well in a general sense. Be prepared to get Lady Luck on your side, particularly if you are planning to take calculated chances. You need enough stimulation today to convince you that you are really giving of your best.

9 MONDAY
Moon Age Day 12   Moon Sign Leo

With everything to play for this is one day during March when you really do need to focus and to put in your best effort. As a reward life should offer you plenty of chances to get ahead and to capitalise on your general level of good luck. You would be wise to concentrate on those areas of life in which you usually excel.

10 TUESDAY
Moon Age Day 13   Moon Sign Virgo

Why not make this a great day for communication, and not just in a verbal sense? Benefits can come from messages of all kinds, and at the same time it's worth keeping up with what is happening in the area where you live. Being in touch with the world also enables you to put yourself in the best possible position to make gains.

11 WEDNESDAY
Moon Age Day 14   Moon Sign Virgo

Trends support a thirst for knowledge and a need to open up your personal horizons, making this an ideal time for travel. Maybe it isn't possible for you to drop everything and fly off to some exotic location, but even small journeys can prove to be a real boon. And even if you can't travel in the flesh, you can do so in your mind.

12 THURSDAY
Moon Age Day 15   Moon Sign Libra

With so much happening in your solar eighth house, be prepared to make use of your need to renovate and even to replace certain things in your life. You can also afford to leave behind old concepts and ideas as you rush on towards all sorts of objectives that perhaps didn't seem important even a few days ago.

13 FRIDAY
Moon Age Day 16   Moon Sign Libra

There is now an even more positive emphasis on communication, and the more you talk to those around you, the greater will be your knowledge of how to react. Right now the spotlight is on your positive talent for saying the right thing at the most opportune time, not to mention your ability to charm the birds from the trees.

14 SATURDAY
Moon Age Day 17   Moon Sign Libra

Be prepared to get some realism into your life, especially as far as home and family are concerned. There are certain aspects of life that cannot be the same as they used to be, and even if it is always comfortable to stick to what you know, altering things for the better can allow you to get into a comfortable rut again for a while.

15 SUNDAY   *Moon Age Day 18   Moon Sign Scorpio*

This is a good time to co-operate, especially regarding plans that take you out of the ordinary and which prevent you from having to follow old or routine patterns of behaviour. Anything that gets you out is well starred on this Sunday, and there are gains to be made from getting to know new people in exciting places.

16 MONDAY   *Moon Age Day 19   Moon Sign Scorpio*

Although it might seem less than likely on a normal working Monday, the planets show that social get-togethers can be particularly rewarding. Maybe these will be after work, but wherever they come from they can help you to bring great joy into your life. Beware of allowing pessimism to creep into your working life or strategies.

17 TUESDAY   *Moon Age Day 20   Moon Sign Sagittarius*

A day to take it slightly easier if you can. There is so much eighth-house activity in your solar chart that you might be inclined to push too hard for change you can't keep up with. Rather than taking on more than you can handle, it's worth learning the art of delegation. Leos can be good at this, but would sometimes rather not bother!

18 WEDNESDAY *Moon Age Day 21   Moon Sign Sagittarius*

This can be a fitting time to improve your personal life, and could be the first occasion in days that you have the chance to stop and notice your nearest and dearest. This can sometimes be a problem for Leo. It isn't that you fail to care, simply that your life becomes so busy you don't spend enough time proving your affection.

19 THURSDAY   *Moon Age Day 22   Moon Sign Capricorn*

Career responsibilities could now offer you many challenges. If life demands leadership and initiative from you, there shouldn't be any problem providing both. You are more than up to any task you choose to take on, though there could be occasions when you are trying to achieve the impossible.

20 FRIDAY
Moon Age Day 23   Moon Sign Capricorn

Cultural matters are boosted by the position of Venus in your solar ninth house. The time is right to find new and interesting things to do, and in order to discover them, all you have to do is to open your eyes. The suggestions of others are certainly worth a second look, and could allow you to create excitement.

21 SATURDAY
Moon Age Day 24   Moon Sign Capricorn

From an emotional point of view a few stresses are possible during the weekend. Before today is out the Moon moves into your opposite sign of Aquarius, and the lunar low will do little to boost either your ego or your confidence. For today your best approach is to keep active and in good company if you can.

22 SUNDAY
Moon Age Day 25   Moon Sign Aquarius

You may now decide that it is difficult to keep up the sort of pace you have been happily maintaining for a couple of weeks. It would be best not to dwell on things today but to jog along happily until you can begin to gain pace once more. You needn't be miserable now, though you can be much more contemplative.

23 MONDAY
Moon Age Day 26   Moon Sign Aquarius

Even if today starts out slowly and without a great deal of promise, by the time the afternoon arrives you can make sure things look and feel quite different. There are potential gains on the financial front, not to mention the chance to bring much-needed attention to something you did a while ago.

24 TUESDAY
Moon Age Day 27   Moon Sign Pisces

This is another good time to eliminate non-essentials and to push forward into uncharted but exciting territory. Leo can be at its best right now, and you have what it takes to turn heads wherever you go. You can also make sure the social scene is especially lively, particularly if you are willing to join in at the drop of a hat.

25 WEDNESDAY   *Moon Age Day 28   Moon Sign Pisces*

This is a period of great enthusiasm, just a little of which could be slightly misplaced. All the same you may not notice your little failures if you are pursuing things to your advantage. The best advice would be to order your routines and do things one at a time, though this may be advice that will fall on deaf ears.

26 THURSDAY   *Moon Age Day 0   Moon Sign Pisces*

Trends encourage you to be a freewheeler today and to do whatever takes your fancy. Unfortunately the responsibilities of life may get in your way. You needn't be put off by this, because in an overall sense you can still push forward and make significant headway. This could be a good day to go shopping.

27 FRIDAY   *Moon Age Day 1   Moon Sign Aries*

You have what it takes to inspire many people, and this is much enhanced by present planetary trends. They could hardly fail to notice your optimistic and sunny nature, which is nearly always present in the case of Leo subjects. Impressing colleagues could also be easy, as will be pleasing those in charge.

28 SATURDAY   *Moon Age Day 2   Moon Sign Aries*

You can afford to take your intellectual development more seriously this weekend and to take on new ideas and possibilities that feed your mind. Of course like everything else this can go too far, and there may be occasions when you overdo things. There is much to be said for meditation too.

29 SUNDAY   *Moon Age Day 3   Moon Sign Taurus*

Even if you have the means to get on well, you could be held back by the limitations that Sunday places upon you. The saying goes that you reap what you sow, and if you have been busy spreading seeds around during the last two weeks or so, you should now be ready to reap the benefits and gains that are available.

30 MONDAY   *Moon Age Day 4   Moon Sign Taurus*

Mars remains in your solar eighth house, and as long as it stays there it supports a definite desire to slough off the old and to make changes to your life that usher in new and exciting potentials. All of this requires energy, and you do need to realise that even you are not immune to exhaustion or simple mental fatigue.

31 TUESDAY   *Moon Age Day 5   Moon Sign Gemini*

Certainly the potential for greater personal freedom is strong, and you have scope to impress others with your ideas for reform and alteration. This can be a fruitful period for travel and for all cultural matters. Nothing might please you more at the moment than to be involved in stimulating conversations with intelligent people.

April

2009

1 WEDNESDAY
Moon Age Day 6   Moon Sign Gemini

You can make yourself the main attraction in social groups, and continue to show how much you have to offer your family and friends. What is most gratifying about this period is that even if you remain generally busy, you can find moments to support and comfort other people. Why not get outings organised now for next weekend?

2 THURSDAY
Moon Age Day 7   Moon Sign Cancer

The Moon is now entering your solar twelfth house, and even if the lunar low didn't slow you down much, this particular trend might. This is a good time for solitude and self-discovery. Instead of doing things today and tomorrow, be prepared to think about the consequences of your actions and the spiritual implications.

3 FRIDAY
Moon Age Day 8   Moon Sign Cancer

Once again trends support a more reserved interlude when you may decide to stay in your own little corner much more than of late. This need not be a problem, and coming ahead of the lunar high, can be a blessing. Small but welcome financial rewards are now possible from a host of directions, some of which are unexpected.

4 SATURDAY
Moon Age Day 9   Moon Sign Leo

You can now get back on form and be prepared to make this an exciting weekend, not simply for yourself but also for those around you. Good fortune is there for the taking under the lunar high, and although the potential may be social rather than professional, you can still exploit the good ideas you have in your head.

5 SUNDAY
Moon Age Day 10   Moon Sign Leo

The time is right to go all out for what you want and to engage in single-minded pursuits. There are gains to be made across the board, particularly in sporting activities. For those Leos who work on a Sunday, you can afford to persuade people higher up the tree than you are to help you out in some way.

6 MONDAY
Moon Age Day 11   Moon Sign Virgo

This is an ideal time to be concentrating on securing a firmer financial footing and for strengthening your sense of security. You will have an advantage at present when it comes to attracting more cash, and you have what it takes to plan effectively. Be prepared to welcome new personalities into your life at any time this week.

7 TUESDAY
Moon Age Day 12   Moon Sign Virgo

There are signs that all sorts of emotions have been brought to the surface recently by Mars in your solar eighth house. This could continue for a while yet, though it shouldn't do you any harm. Your strength lies in looking at past situations again in the light of present experience – which is really just a learning process.

8 WEDNESDAY
Moon Age Day 13   Moon Sign Virgo

A diversity of interests would suit you best around the middle of this week, rather than simply concentrating on the practical aspects of life. Don't be afraid to let your mind wander a little, because although you can't afford to take your eye off the ball in practical matters, you can still enjoy some mental freedom.

9 THURSDAY
Moon Age Day 14   Moon Sign Libra

There is much to be said for remaining active today and trying to learn things that could be of use to you in the future. This would be a very good time for educating yourself through travel or as a result of things you read. Even if not everyone agrees with your logic at this time, in the end you have to make up your own mind.

10 FRIDAY
Moon Age Day 15   Moon Sign Libra

Trends encourage you to experiment all the time. That's fine, because it is part of what makes you wiser, but you may need to be careful that other people don't feel you are manipulating them for your own ends. If you remain sensitive to those around you this shouldn't happen, and you should have scope to proceed as you wish.

11 SATURDAY
Moon Age Day 16   Moon Sign Scorpio

The Moon in your solar fourth house is an ideal time to make the best of family and domestic matters. Although this needn't be a stay-at-home sort of weekend, it might be a chance for discussions with family members. Maybe you are taking some of them along with you on an adventure, and the change would do everyone good.

12 SUNDAY
Moon Age Day 17   Moon Sign Scorpio

Now is the time to give joint finances a boost, even if you think that things are looking a bit gloomy on the money front. Perhaps there is something you have forgotten that can be used to your advantage, or maybe you can find ways to draw on new resources and therefore feel more secure.

13 MONDAY
Moon Age Day 18   Moon Sign Sagittarius

Discovering the lively and sparkling side of your personality is as easy as simply being yourself today. In almost all circumstances you have what it takes to shine like a star and to get those around you to notice. Positive comments from others can allow you to bolster your own self-esteem.

14 TUESDAY
Moon Age Day 19   Moon Sign Sagittarius

Be prepared to find ways to further advance your intellect, perhaps by taking on new educational initiatives. Even if you can get others to see you as attractive, clever and dynamic, there may be things within yourself that you still want to change. One thing at once is the best key to success, even for a Leo.

15 WEDNESDAY   *Moon Age Day 20   Moon Sign Sagittarius*

The emphasis turns to emotional relationships now that Venus is in your solar sixth house. What is on offer is a greater sense of security within romantic and family ties, and the chance to appreciate that those you care about the most are doing what they can for you. It's a process of sharing that enables you to achieve a warm glow.

16 THURSDAY   *Moon Age Day 21   Moon Sign Capricorn*

You work very well at the moment when sorting and analysing is necessary. This is an ideal time for developing practical methods and routines, and for getting everything in its place, especially at work. When it comes to your social life, things could be rather more chaotic, but perhaps that's the way you like it!

17 FRIDAY   *Moon Age Day 22   Moon Sign Capricorn*

Whilst the Sun remains in your solar ninth house you are encouraged to learn and to increase the level of your intelligence. Your interests are best served by mixing with people you find stimulating and intellectually motivated, and you probably won't take kindly to rude, crude or plainly ignorant types.

18 SATURDAY   *Moon Age Day 23   Moon Sign Aquarius*

Unexpected delays could be a consequence of the lunar low this month. The fact that the Moon is in Aquarius at the weekend might tell its own tale, particularly if you find yourself hemmed in by domestic requirements or simple routines. The best way forward is to relax, and to be willing to look for a little assistance.

19 SUNDAY   *Moon Age Day 24   Moon Sign Aquarius*

Be prepared to do a little serious thinking today, especially about work. If you aren't at your adventurous or most energetic best right now, you may as well save this time specifically for planning. As far as the more practical aspects of life are concerned, why not learn a little patience and let them wait for another day?

20 MONDAY   *Moon Age Day 25   Moon Sign Aquarius*

Although the Moon is still in Aquarius when you begin the new working week, it doesn't stay there for very long. You can get yourself back on form by the afternoon and show an unsuspecting world what you are capable of doing. Any mental challenges that you avoided during the weekend could now become child's play.

21 TUESDAY   *Moon Age Day 26   Moon Sign Pisces*

Mars has now moved out of your solar eighth house, after a fairly protracted period there. You may well notice that some tension has been released, and you mightn't be quite so inclined to overthrow everything in an attempt to start from scratch all the time. A more concentrated and potentially successful period is at hand.

22 WEDNESDAY   *Moon Age Day 27   Moon Sign Pisces*

Today the Sun enters your solar tenth house, allowing you to capitalise on a fairly progressive time for the next three or four weeks. New possibilities are there for the taking from a variety of different directions, and you should be in a position to make gains, especially at work. Be prepared to deal with awkward attitudes from others.

23 THURSDAY   *Moon Age Day 28   Moon Sign Aries*

Your strength now lies in looking at the big picture, and in using opportunities to get ahead. Beware of taking up every offer that comes along, otherwise you will crowd your schedule too much. The secret of today is knowing which direction to take and which circumstances to leave well alone.

24 FRIDAY   *Moon Age Day 29   Moon Sign Aries*

A great time for career discussions and for deciding exactly what you are going to do across the next few months. Some Leos could be on the verge of advancement and a few might even be thinking about an entirely new start in terms of career. The time is right to seek out people around who can help.

25 SATURDAY   *Moon Age Day 0   Moon Sign Taurus*

The focus is on learning more at the moment, and you also have a tremendous capacity for seeing beyond the next horizon. Even if others get lost in the details of life, you can push right through and achieve bigger and better objectives. Expanding your wisdom and insight will assist you to give advice to others.

26 SUNDAY   *Moon Age Day 1   Moon Sign Taurus*

This may be one of the best days of the month as far as general progress is concerned, and the only stumbling point could be that these trends come along on a Sunday. The result may be frustration, particularly if you can't make use of as many opportunities as you might wish. If you can't run the entire show, that could annoy you.

27 MONDAY   *Moon Age Day 2   Moon Sign Gemini*

It is an innate ability of Leo to bring out the best in others, and this could well be the case today. You can put your talents to good use as far as your career is concerned, as well as to resolve any complications in your personal life. A less stressed Leo should be apparent today.

28 TUESDAY   *Moon Age Day 3   Moon Sign Gemini*

Today you can find ways to release the tremendous reservoir of energy that you have available. This is a good time to throw yourself fully into changes and alterations to your life that you know are going to be positive. You can also direct energy to your social life, perhaps by doing things that others find terrifying!

29 WEDNESDAY   *Moon Age Day 4   Moon Sign Cancer*

An ideal day to spend time on spiritual interests, because this is a part of your life that cannot be ignored, no matter how busy you may be. It's worth taking time out to look at the changing face of nature, read an inspirational poem or indulge in a little positive nostalgia. You have to learn that not everything is founded in physical activity.

30 THURSDAY

Moon Age Day 5   Moon Sign Cancer

Venus, now in your solar ninth house, assists you to create excitement and make contact with people who may be inspirational to your future. Your need to break the bounds of convention is highlighted, and though this is not necessarily a bad thing, it's worth making sure you don't get on the wrong side of people who matter.

May

2009

1 FRIDAY
Moon Age Day 6   Moon Sign Cancer

You can get ahead today as a result of the very real effort you are willing to put into everything you do. Money matters are well starred, and you also have what it takes to get on very well as far as your romantic life is concerned. By tomorrow you can improve things even more, but even today you should be on a roll.

2 SATURDAY
Moon Age Day 7   Moon Sign Leo

Helping others is part of what the lunar high is about, and you have scope to make yourself flavour of the month. You can use your popularity to get ahead better and especially so if you work at the weekend. Be prepared to find some space to do whatever takes your fancy and then put in maximum effort.

3 SUNDAY
Moon Age Day 8   Moon Sign Leo

This is a Sunday that could go down in the diary as having been extra special. A host of planetary influences are presently available to help you make progress, whatever your level of effort. Make the most of the positive attention you can attract from others. Remember that financial benefits are not the only gains to be made.

4 MONDAY
Moon Age Day 9   Moon Sign Virgo

The time is right to be optimistic and adventurous, and to use these traits to get to the end of a specific objective that you think has been waiting in the wings for too long. You would be wise to avoid rushing things too much, and a little caution would be advisable today no matter what you decide to do.

5 TUESDAY   *Moon Age Day 10   Moon Sign Virgo*

Daily outings and even long-distance travel are well starred at this time, and you can achieve a great deal by putting yourself in the way of success, rather than by just hoping for it. Even little things can mean a lot to your nearest and dearest, so why not put aside some time to give them some positive attention?

6 WEDNESDAY   *Moon Age Day 11   Moon Sign Libra*

There is increased energy on offer whilst the Sun remains in your solar tenth house, and you can use it to get things working out to your advantage more than you might have expected. A day for keeping in touch with people, no matter what means you use to do so. Be prepared to capitalise on any unusual happenings.

7 THURSDAY   ☿   *Moon Age Day 12   Moon Sign Libra*

Don't allow unnecessary arguments to crop up, and avoid getting on the wrong side of those who could be in the best position to support your present ideas. You can afford to modify your stance regarding a family matter, and to reap the benefits that such a compromise can bring.

8 FRIDAY   ☿   *Moon Age Day 13   Moon Sign Scorpio*

A day to take a close look at the domestic scene and to spend time with family members, especially your partner. It might seem as though there are few moments to spare in your busy schedule, but you can always fit in some quality time with those you love. Under present trends this can mean a great deal.

9 SATURDAY   ☿   *Moon Age Day 14   Moon Sign Scorpio*

A fresh boost to love and romantic matters generally is support by the present position of the Moon. You have scope to take a starring role in life around this time and to give of your best, particularly in social situations. Remember that saying and doing the right thing can help you to boost your popularity no end.

10 SUNDAY   ☿   *Moon Age Day 15*   *Moon Sign Scorpio*

What you are doing in a moment-by-moment sense might seem to be under scrutiny from others. If this really is the case, make sure that they will see your actions in a favourable light, and that you are able to attract powerful new friends. Any personality clashes at home can be rectified with a little tolerance all round.

11 MONDAY   ☿ *Moon Age Day 16*   *Moon Sign Sagittarius*

In a social sense you have a chance to branch out this week and needn't be specifically tied to doing those things that routine demands. On the contrary, the time is right to break down the bounds of the commonplace and pursue some variety. You can use your silver tongue to talk others round to your way of thinking.

12 TUESDAY   ☿ *Moon Age Day 17*   *Moon Sign Sagittarius*

Trends support a very strong urge for freedom, and you may not take kindly to others telling you what you have to do. Of course there are times when this is inevitable, especially at work. You won't do yourself any favours if you stick out for independence at all costs, so it's worth considering a compromise.

13 WEDNESDAY ☿ *Moon Age Day 18*   *Moon Sign Capricorn*

Instead of being on the move again, today is ideal for sticking around and getting on with any jobs that have been piling up. Efficiency is the key at the moment, and you can use it to get to grips with tasks you have been studiously avoiding. Be prepared to glean some intriguing information from friends.

14 THURSDAY ☿ *Moon Age Day 19*   *Moon Sign Capricorn*

This could be a very good day for voicing new ideas and for introducing altered schedules. You can afford to be flexible in your attitude and to be willing to see another point of view. Your strength lies in your sunny and optimistic nature, which you can use to attract others and to increase your popularity.

15 FRIDAY ☿ *Moon Age Day 20   Moon Sign Capricorn*

Trends encourage a curiosity to know how something beneath the surface is working out, so don't be afraid to do a little detective work around now. By all means burn the candle at both ends, though this may become more difficult by tomorrow. A sense of proportion is important where cash is concerned.

16 SATURDAY ☿ *Moon Age Day 21   Moon Sign Aquarius*

Some setbacks and alterations are possible whilst the lunar low is around, but this doesn't mean you have to stop trying. Be prepared to pace yourself and also allow others to do something on your behalf. After all, if you work hard on their account, you should be able to get them to lend you a hand on occasion.

17 SUNDAY ☿ *Moon Age Day 22   Moon Sign Aquarius*

Even if you are feeling slightly insecure around now, there is really no reason why this should be the case. Compromise may not be easy in personal attachments, and life could seem just a little messy at times. By tomorrow you should have an opportunity to resolve many of your present concerns.

18 MONDAY ☿ *Moon Age Day 23   Moon Sign Pisces*

The Moon has now moved on and should prove to be in a particularly good position when it comes to supporting your personal and romantic life. If you let your smile return, it should be easier to bring pleasure into the lives of most people you encounter. A cheery hello is all it takes.

19 TUESDAY ☿ *Moon Age Day 24   Moon Sign Pisces*

Large enterprises or work on a scale you haven't encountered for a while could prove to be fortuitous and could offer the chance to achieve a level of success that has been rare in recent times. Why not review some of the ideas that have occurred to you in the past? After all, they may now be more attainable.

20 WEDNESDAY ☿ · *Moon Age Day 25* · *Moon Sign Aries*

All of a sudden, trends encourage you to be on the move. It may not be enough simply to think about travel – you might feel the urge to get on a train or a plane. If this isn't possible, it's still worth thinking up something to break the routines and any monotony you are presently feeling. All it takes is some imagination.

21 THURSDAY ☿ · *Moon Age Day 26* · *Moon Sign Aries*

Today is good for communicating with others and is made all the better by the position of Venus in your solar ninth house. Now is the time to use your personal magnetism to get on very well with people from all walks of life. Be prepared to welcome someone you haven't seen for some time back into your life.

22 FRIDAY ☿ · *Moon Age Day 27* · *Moon Sign Aries*

There is strong optimism that you can achieve anything you decide to undertake today. Your strength lies in making make progress with new ideas and not taking no for an answer if you have made your mind up about anything. This could make you slightly more awkward to deal with around now!

23 SATURDAY ☿ · *Moon Age Day 28* · *Moon Sign Taurus*

The spotlight is now on personal issues, and this is a weekend when you have a chance to look at relationships full on and close. Are things going the way you would wish? That is the question to ask yourself, and if the answer is 'no', you may need to alter certain situations. Friendships and group activities are well accented.

24 SUNDAY ☿ · *Moon Age Day 0* · *Moon Sign Taurus*

Social and teamwork matters are now even more highly emphasised than was the case yesterday. If you are a sporting Leo, today could offer the chance of success, especially in terms of team or contact sports. In a more practical sense, it's worth reminding yourself that everything that glistens is not gold.

25 MONDAY ☿ *Moon Age Day 1   Moon Sign Gemini*

At the start of a new working week there is much to be said for turning your present co-operative frame of mind in the direction of your work. You have scope to persuade people to fall in line with your ideas and methods, particularly if you manage to put your point of view across in a more diplomatic way.

26 TUESDAY ☿ *Moon Age Day 2   Moon Sign Gemini*

Don't be afraid to focus on your inner life for a while and look carefully at your deepest thoughts and emotions. This is an ideal time to work out how your actions can have a bearing on the lives of those around you. Trends enhance your concern not only for your immediate circle but also for your country and planet.

27 WEDNESDAY ☿ *Moon Age Day 3   Moon Sign Cancer*

In a social sense you can now be on the up and up. You have scope to put thoughts of work and responsibility to one side as you work on new ways of mixing and having fun. This is so much a part of the Leo nature that it isn't especially surprising. What might be astonishing is the response you get from adversaries.

28 THURSDAY ☿ *Moon Age Day 4   Moon Sign Cancer*

A very slightly quieter Leo could well be on display immediately ahead of the lunar high. A more withdrawn approach works best, though not to the extent that anyone is likely to notice too much change. Minor but potentially important financial rewards are possible, though it's important to use any money in a very wise way.

29 FRIDAY ☿ *Moon Age Day 5   Moon Sign Leo*

In a professional sense you shouldn't have to look all that hard for success whilst the lunar high is around, though it's also worth focusing your attention on your personal and social life. Anything that means positive change and interaction with others is grist to your mill, and you have what it takes to move forward with great hope.

30 SATURDAY ☿ *Moon Age Day 6   Moon Sign Leo*

Put your luck to the test this weekend and watch how things begin to pan out positively for you. This is not a day to be stuck in the shadows or to remain within your own four walls. If you want to make the best of the lunar high, be prepared to be out there pitching. If that means putting yourself on display, so much the better!

31 SUNDAY ☿ *Moon Age Day 7   Moon Sign Virgo*

Even though the Moon has moved on, you needn't lose your sense of freedom. This isn't a time to be restricted in your movements, though it's worth letting others know that you don't intend to be stuck in the same place. The best way to achieve your objectives now is to search for them.

2009

1 MONDAY
Moon Age Day 8   Moon Sign Virgo

While you weren't looking the Sun moved on from your tenth to your solar eleventh house, bringing a slight change of emphasis. For the next few weeks you have scope to discover even more social highlights and a greater commitment to mixing business with pleasure. Your strength lies in making life more interesting.

2 TUESDAY
Moon Age Day 9   Moon Sign Libra

You needn't complain that life is boring right now. In fact, the opposite could be the case, and there is much to be said for slowing things down a little. Even if you aren't becoming fatigued, you could be losing touch with specific possibilities because you can't keep so many balls in the air at the same time.

3 WEDNESDAY
Moon Age Day 10   Moon Sign Libra

Information exchange is the key around now, not just for your own sake but for that of the people with whom you live and work. Everyone has good ideas from time to time, and it's worth picking the brains of even the most unlikely people today. The time is right to keep your ears open and share what you know with them.

4 THURSDAY
Moon Age Day 11   Moon Sign Scorpio

The spotlight is now on your home life, thanks to a fourth-house Moon. If there are certain family members who are coming to a very important stage in their lives, why not offer them help and advice? Whatever is going on, you have what it takes to show great support and to give all the assistance you can.

5 FRIDAY
Moon Age Day 12   Moon Sign Scorpio

Trends highlight your need to do things your own way at this time, and you may not take kindly to toeing a line that others have set. On the contrary, you can afford to fight like mad to have your own way and to take responsibility for the ground rules. Extra work might be necessary today to fulfil a promise or to prepare for later.

6 SATURDAY
Moon Age Day 13   Moon Sign Scorpio

Today is a bonus as far as personal attachments are concerned. Romance is definitely emphasised, and those Leo people who have been looking for new love should concentrate their efforts around now. In most situations an idealistic approach is favoured, and you needn't compromise your principles – no matter what.

7 SUNDAY
Moon Age Day 14   Moon Sign Sagittarius

Get things in order today! This isn't usually very necessary for the Lion, but you can achieve more at present if you know exactly what you are up against. Wherever you are today, sorting things out counts for a great deal now. The time is right to do something that makes you feel tidier and more 'in the know'.

8 MONDAY
Moon Age Day 15   Moon Sign Sagittarius

There are gains to be made through associating with people who give you encouragement and new incentives, rather than with those who insist on being pessimistic. More than usual you are now very susceptible to atmospheres, and would be wise to seek out the most positive company that life can offer you.

9 TUESDAY
Moon Age Day 16   Moon Sign Capricorn

There is much to be done at the moment, and the only potential problem is whether or not you have sufficient time to fit it all in. You can achieve a fairly positive time on the relationship front, and could also use this interlude to make new friends. If there is something you really want today, have the cheek to ask for it!

10 WEDNESDAY   *Moon Age Day 17   Moon Sign Capricorn*

Be prepared to show a little will-power and curb any tendency to do anything to excess. Some Leo people will be starting a health kick around now and if you are one of them just remember to proceed with caution instead of knocking yourself out on the first day. Rules and regulations mightn't appeal at this time.

11 THURSDAY   *Moon Age Day 18   Moon Sign Capricorn*

The generally positive interlude continues, and you might also notice all sorts of strange little coincidences. Many of these can act as signposts to point you in the right direction, though some might seem distinctly odd. It's worth seeking out support for a planned change at work, particularly if it's you who is doing the planning.

12 FRIDAY   *Moon Age Day 19   Moon Sign Aquarius*

The power you have to change things in your life may be limited while the lunar low is around, and there are times today when your best approach is to settle for second-best. Even if you want to be at the centre of things, you can only make the best of the prevailing situations. Accolades may be hard to achieve today.

13 SATURDAY   *Moon Age Day 20   Moon Sign Aquarius*

Current plans of action will need some thinking about, particularly under the lunar low. This gives you more time to sort situations out in your mind, and to consider every angle before you speak. By tomorrow you can get yourself right back on form, but for the moment an element of confusion is possible.

14 SUNDAY   *Moon Age Day 21   Moon Sign Pisces*

A hectic trend that begins today is inspired by the position of Mercury in your solar chart. This assists you to keep on the move, and today might seem even more frenetic if it follows on from a couple of quiet days. Be prepared to focus on potential accomplishments and future plans, and to deal with demands on your time.

15 MONDAY *Moon Age Day 22   Moon Sign Pisces*

With sufficient insight you can solve tough problems and persuade others to follow your lead. In a personal sense you also have what it takes to turn heads, and so can ensure that popularity is part of the scenario right now. You achieve a really good understanding of what makes those around you tick, and that can be useful.

16 TUESDAY *Moon Age Day 23   Moon Sign Pisces*

Continuing on a generally positive journey through life, you have scope to achieve more in the way of professional advancement, as well as accolades from people in positions of authority. Even if you are more than justifying your position at work, don't be afraid to think about home-based matters as well.

17 WEDNESDAY *Moon Age Day 24   Moon Sign Aries*

An ideal day to look up old social contacts and maybe to go right back into the past in one way or another. Perhaps you are thinking about old school friends and potential reunions – or else those individuals who had a great part to play in your younger days. Nostalgia is part of what today is about, and that's quite unusual for you.

18 THURSDAY *Moon Age Day 25   Moon Sign Aries*

When it comes to general developments in life there is really nobody about to beat you. Trends support dynamic actions, and thought processes that are clear and concise. Whilst other people are thinking about doing something, you can have it finished and be well on with the next task. Progress is within your grasp.

19 FRIDAY *Moon Age Day 26   Moon Sign Taurus*

A little charm and persuasion can get you almost anything you want today. Don't forget it's the last day of the working week, and it's worth putting something into operation that will mature after the weekend. Leaving things until later just isn't the best way to function under current planetary influences.

20 SATURDAY · · · · · · · · · · · · *Moon Age Day 27 · · · Moon Sign Taurus*

The time is right for some give and take, though there may be occasions when you expect more give from others and consequently more take from you. Don't be too quick to dismiss any accusations of selfishness. By all means get your own way, but do it kindly and diplomatically.

21 SUNDAY · · · · · · · · · · · · · · *Moon Age Day 28 · · · Moon Sign Gemini*

Getting ahead at this time is really down to the number of contacts you have in life. Because you are a Leo there could well be many, some of whom are simply friends or acquaintances. You can now persuade just about any of your associates to lend you a timely hand, and may also decide that professional advice would be helpful.

22 MONDAY · · · · · · · · · · · · · · *Moon Age Day 29 · · · Moon Sign Gemini*

Your sensitivity is enhanced, and now that the Sun is in your solar twelfth house a slightly more reclusive interlude is a distinct possibility. In the main this trend is hardly noticeable for a Leo, but may show itself in all manner of ways today. Be prepared to direct your thoughts to those who are less well off than you.

23 TUESDAY · · · · · · · · · · · · · · · *Moon Age Day 0 · · · Moon Sign Cancer*

Test your good luck today, because although the Moon doesn't move into your zodiac sign until Thursday, you have scope to make positive things happen. Perhaps you are simply in the best place to make headway, or it could be that you are thinking things through carefully. Don't get hung up on details when at work.

24 WEDNESDAY · · · · · · · · · · · · *Moon Age Day 1 · · · Moon Sign Cancer*

Career rewards can now be achieved through the recognition others have of your professionalism and your sense of fair play. You have what it takes to impress those who can do you some good, and to respond extremely positively in most situations. An ideal day to find something you've been looking for.

25 THURSDAY
Moon Age Day 2   Moon Sign Leo

Certain goals and objectives should be much easier to achieve whilst the lunar high is around. There is little to hold you back and everything to play for, especially when it comes to love and romance. Set out your stall to be a winner because that's the way the world sees you. You can also make up your own rules today and tomorrow.

26 FRIDAY
Moon Age Day 3   Moon Sign Leo

If your personal standing is high, that should breed ever more confidence. In a general sense you can forge ahead, but the best area of life at this time is probably that associated with personal and romantic matters. Your have what it takes to give the words of love you utter today a poetic appeal that others can't ignore.

27 SATURDAY
Moon Age Day 4   Moon Sign Virgo

Under the surface trends encourage you to meditate, and assist you to take things in your stride. Spiritual matters are well starred whilst the Sun is in your solar twelfth house, and you can afford to spend more time than usual wondering what life is really all about. There may be no answer, but it's fun to look!

28 SUNDAY
Moon Age Day 5   Moon Sign Virgo

Venus is now in your solar tenth house and this can be extremely useful when it comes to getting others to do your bidding. You can achieve this without putting any undue stress upon them, and you have what it takes to make those around you very relaxed. This suits your present attitude and your contemplative mood.

29 MONDAY
Moon Age Day 6   Moon Sign Libra

A day to show off your leadership skills to the full and to make this the start of a very positive sort of week. Your strength lies in the attention you can attract from people who are in a position to enhance your working life, and in your willingness to make the most of educational opportunities. Beware of internalising worries.

30 TUESDAY

Moon Age Day 7   Moon Sign Libra

You would be wise to avoid self-deception or any escapist tendencies, and to stick to what you know in a practical sense. There are times when you may feel disorganised or unclear about the way things are going in a general sense. However, you needn't allow such interludes to get in your way too much.

July

2009

1 WEDNESDAY
Moon Age Day 8   Moon Sign Libra

Though present trends tempt you to be rather easy-going about work and life generally, you can ensure that professional matters at least are running fairly smoothly at the beginning of this month. Today offers you the chance to make life work more to your advantage, and to achieve happiness as a result.

2 THURSDAY
Moon Age Day 9   Moon Sign Scorpio

The focus is on domestic responsibilities at this time, and it could be that you are so busy considering what is happening at home that you have less time than you would wish for the practical aspects of life. In some ways your nature is torn at the moment, so be prepared to deal with frustration in a measured way.

3 FRIDAY
Moon Age Day 10   Moon Sign Scorpio

Today works best if you go with the flow and don't try to force anything. Let go of old attachments if they no longer seem to be serving any realistic purpose in your life, and maybe have a sort out of those overcrowded wardrobes. Even if confidence isn't at an all-time high, you can at least gain encouragement from other people.

4 SATURDAY
Moon Age Day 11   Moon Sign Sagittarius

Capitalise on one of the best times of the month for putting yourself in the social limelight and for making the best of impressions on the world at large. You can also put your creative talents to the test and at the same time encourage others to make more of their own gifts. This is an altogether co-operative sort of day.

5 SUNDAY   *Moon Age Day 12   Moon Sign Sagittarius*

Rather than being preoccupied with specific matters, it's worth looking at the wider spectrum of life. Circumstances could conspire to put you on some sort of pedestal in the estimation of those around you, and even if an elevated position is usually what you seek, this may not be the case under present planetary trends.

6 MONDAY   *Moon Age Day 13   Moon Sign Sagittarius*

At work this has potential to be a fairly quiet period, offering you an opportunity to think about things more deeply. Trends encourage a contemplative approach for the first couple of days this week, and you may decide not to rush at anything. You can afford to spend some time enjoying the summer weather.

7 TUESDAY   *Moon Age Day 14   Moon Sign Capricorn*

Be prepared to seek out new friends or social contacts that haven't shown themselves before. The time is right to make the most of chance meetings and unusual happenings to register your own progress in life, and also to find the necessary time to prove to your partner or sweetheart how important they are.

8 WEDNESDAY   *Moon Age Day 15   Moon Sign Capricorn*

Your ability to be practical and also efficient may be hampered for the next few days. Even if you start out fine, by this afternoon the lunar low could begin to have a bearing on your life. Why not spend some time alone and think things through quietly? That's what the lunar low is really all about.

9 THURSDAY   *Moon Age Day 16   Moon Sign Aquarius*

You might still not be making very much progress in a practical sense, but there is, after all, more to life than getting things done. Now you can enjoy time spent with loved ones or friends, soaking up the summer and really noticing what is taking place around you all the time. Don't get frustrated by minor obstacles.

10 FRIDAY *Moon Age Day 17 Moon Sign Aquarius*

It might still be difficult to get your ideas across to others, and you may well decide not to try to do so, at least until tomorrow. You can afford to be quite happy in your own little world and to avoid pitching yourself against what can seem like a harsh world. You can use your accustomed Leo fortitude again tomorrow.

11 SATURDAY *Moon Age Day 18 Moon Sign Aquarius*

Life may still not be doing you any favours, at least at the start of today, but you can change this state of affairs quickly enough as Saturday wears on. Now is the time to confront situations and to get yourself back in the social mainstream. The good ideas of friends are worth a second glance.

12 SUNDAY *Moon Age Day 19 Moon Sign Pisces*

Your intuition plays a greater part in your life at the moment, and if something just doesn't seem to be the way it appears, it's worth stopping and taking note. You can do yourself all sorts of favours right now by simply being in the right place at the best time to act. There is a much more decisive quality about you from today on.

13 MONDAY *Moon Age Day 20 Moon Sign Pisces*

Mars is now in your solar eleventh house, and fits of temper could be a definite possibility. This is particularly relevant if those around you seem to be deliberately stupid. There are certainly occasions now when you may decide it is easier simply to do things for yourself.

14 TUESDAY *Moon Age Day 21 Moon Sign Aries*

Be prepared to allow your attitude to grow more expansive and to try new things simply for the sake of seeing what the results might be. You have what it takes to be experimental in your approach to life and can use this trait to find out how and why everything is the way it is. You needn't be deterred by the attitude of others.

15 WEDNESDAY   *Moon Age Day 22   Moon Sign Aries*

The Sun remains in your solar twelfth house, where it has now been for the last three weeks or so. This still supports a more withdrawn interlude when you may be less inclined to push yourself forward than would normally be the case. The period ends early next week, so don't despair if you are starting to feel something like a hermit.

16 THURSDAY   *Moon Age Day 23   Moon Sign Taurus*

Being ambitious and hard working comes quite naturally to Leo, and even if you are feeling slightly detached and withdrawn, that needn't be how things appear to those who watch you. To them you can still be go-getting and ambitious. An ideal time to seek help from colleagues, and to try to mix business with pleasure.

17 FRIDAY   *Moon Age Day 24   Moon Sign Taurus*

Allowing the tempo of life to be flexible would be no bad thing, and should avoid the build-up of tension. The Sun encourages you to slow down, whilst other planets and your own natural instincts support you in pushing forward. If this becomes difficult, your best approach would be to divide up your day somewhat.

18 SATURDAY   *Moon Age Day 25   Moon Sign Taurus*

Friendships are now much enhanced and you may feel inspired by a sense of social equality. It is now only a few days until the Sun moves on in your chart, and at that time you can capitalise on the most progressive period of the year. In the meantime, enjoyment is the order of the day, though probably in a relaxed and subdued way.

19 SUNDAY   *Moon Age Day 26   Moon Sign Gemini*

One of your greatest gifts is your ability to motivate others. This is much emphasised at the moment, assisting you to get the very best out of family members and friends, but especially your life partner. The focus is also on luck, so don't be afraid to indulge in a little speculation.

20 MONDAY   *Moon Age Day 27   Moon Sign Gemini*

Mercury now enters your solar first house, a herald of all that is going to take place in this part of your solar chart across the next few weeks. It encourages you to stop and take note more, and also supports a chattier approach. If you make sure you are fun to have around, the social invitations should roll in!

21 TUESDAY   *Moon Age Day 28   Moon Sign Cancer*

Beware of allowing emotions to govern your actions today, which is what is possible with the Moon and the Sun in your twelfth house. This is the last gasp of a solar position that probably doesn't suit you at all, and you should be able to increase your level of happiness in the days ahead. For the moment, try to stay on the level.

22 WEDNESDAY   *Moon Age Day 0   Moon Sign Cancer*

Today the Sun enters your solar first house and for you in particular this is very important. The Sun is your ruling planet and represents the essence of vitality to Leo. Be prepared to change your general attitude to life and to make the most of your luck and popularity. After all, these come from your own actions.

23 THURSDAY   *Moon Age Day 1   Moon Sign Leo*

Not only is the Sun now in your solar first house but the Moon is there too. This can be the day of days for many Leo subjects, and if you aren't making headway now, you are probably not trying as hard as you could. Grasp every opportunity and insist that people do things your way. Good luck is also there for the taking.

24 FRIDAY   *Moon Age Day 2   Moon Sign Leo*

This has potential to be an industrious time and one during which you can get the forces of life flowing your way. The end of the working week could offer some pleasant surprises and the chance to show your charms. After a month during which circumstances have not assisted progress, you can now get them going your way.

25 SATURDAY
Moon Age Day 3   Moon Sign Virgo

A day to get out in front and be very personable. Whatever opportunities come your way, you are in a position to jump on them immediately and to take advantage of the good nature and help of those around you. At home you have scope to show your warm and caring side, and to enjoy the love that you can attract.

26 SUNDAY
Moon Age Day 4   Moon Sign Virgo

This is another great day for getting involved and for being the natural leader that your star sign assists you to be. Even if you are participating in group activities, you have what it takes to put yourself in command, and that means you can have things very much your own way. Finances are also well starred.

27 MONDAY
Moon Age Day 5   Moon Sign Libra

Talking and listening are to the fore in equal measure today and you should be able to move your own plans forward to a much greater extent than seems to have been the case across the last few weeks. You can further enhance the start of this working week by using good news on the professional front together with a little romance!

28 TUESDAY
Moon Age Day 6   Moon Sign Libra

Your capacity to focus all the energy you presently feel is what helps you to get on well at the moment. Capitalise on your sense of freedom by taking any opportunity to travel and to see new places. You can ensure that most experiences are positive ones, and you needn't be afraid to tell everyone about them.

29 WEDNESDAY
Moon Age Day 7   Moon Sign Scorpio

Those Leo people who have chosen this time to take a holiday could be the luckiest of all, but even if you can't get away for days on end you ought to be able to arrange short outings. You need to look at the world on its own doorstep at this time, and simply flicking through travel brochures may not be enough.

30 THURSDAY   *Moon Age Day 8   Moon Sign Scorpio*

If social issues look settled and happy, you might have more time and greater incentive to make new friends and to avoid any sort of disagreement with others. General confidence is also highlighted, assisting you to do the right thing under almost all circumstances – though do be wary of get-rich-quick schemes.

31 FRIDAY   *Moon Age Day 9   Moon Sign Sagittarius*

A day on which you may be swept up with your own enthusiasm more than is good for you. Your best approach is to make sure that what you promise to deliver is realistic and that you don't take on more than is practical. It would be far better to do a couple of things really well than to approach a dozen tasks in a shoddy way.

August

2009

1 SATURDAY   Moon Age Day 10   Moon Sign Sagittarius

The emphasis is much more on fun and self-expression this weekend than on responsibility. Why not let others take the strain whilst you have fun with people you find great to have around? Wide-open spaces and plenty of fresh air can help you to feed your zest for life in the best way that proves to be possible.

2 SUNDAY   Moon Age Day 11   Moon Sign Sagittarius

Trends today encourage practical thinking, with a veneer of common sense to protect you against trying too hard in the wrong direction. Your intuition is also favoured, a factor that should stand you in good stead for dealing with dubious types or situations with which you are unfamiliar.

3 MONDAY   Moon Age Day 12   Moon Sign Capricorn

Meeting new people can help to keep you stimulated at the moment and you should also be in a position to make greater headway in your work. The time is right to seek out like-minded people and swap ideas with them. They say great minds think alike, but remember that differences can also breed success.

4 TUESDAY   Moon Age Day 13   Moon Sign Capricorn

This has potential to be an easy-going phase, assisting you to get things running in a very smooth way. There are possible gains to be made where money is concerned, and you need to make the most of new opportunities that are available. Take advantage of the co-operative tendencies of family members.

5 WEDNESDAY   *Moon Age Day 14   Moon Sign Aquarius*

It is just possible that your expectations could be too high for the next two or three days. The lunar low comes as the first stumbling block since the Sun moved into Leo, and it's worth being a little wary of doing more than is strictly necessary. Your love life is well accented at present, with romantic attention available if you seek it.

6 THURSDAY   *Moon Age Day 15   Moon Sign Aquarius*

This is not the best time for business initiatives, but is an ideal period for enjoying what your home life and personal attachments have to offer. Rather than trying to achieve too much, be prepared to consolidate. It won't do you any harm to stick fast for a while, though nothing need prevent your mind from being progressive.

7 FRIDAY   *Moon Age Day 16   Moon Sign Aquarius*

Close partnerships are what can make life really fulfilling right now. The Moon moves on later today, allowing you to get back to being the driving, seeking individual that you naturally represent. All the same you should still find time to prove to others how important they are and how much you love them.

8 SATURDAY   *Moon Age Day 17   Moon Sign Pisces*

With the Sun still in your sign you can afford to have a strong faith in yourself and your own abilities. If you remain confident, you can persuade others to accept your point of view in most things, and that helps you to get your own way. Don't give up, even when the going gets tough. Use your charms to the full.

9 SUNDAY   *Moon Age Day 18   Moon Sign Pisces*

Love life and relationships generally may be slightly harder work today. Although the Sun and Mercury are now rooting for you in your solar first house, Venus remains in your twelfth house, which is not ideal. Maybe you just can't get your lover to feel about something the way you do. A little extra patience can work wonders.

10 MONDAY · Moon Age Day 19 · Moon Sign Aries

Your ordered mind can assist you to seek success in business matters this week. Even if dealing with awkward types gets in your way today, in the main you have what it takes to brush any problems aside. This might not be so easy in matters associated with romance, because here diplomacy and tact are necessary.

11 TUESDAY · Moon Age Day 20 · Moon Sign Aries

Trends now support some touchiness in your dealings with the world at large, and since this is so unlike you it could well come as a shock to some of the people around you. You can blame Mars in your eleventh house for this, though there are some strong supporting planets around too and these offer you a calmer approach.

12 WEDNESDAY · Moon Age Day 21 · Moon Sign Aries

It's one thing scoring points in specific situations, but something else completely to feel secure in your life and especially in your professional position. Your best approach at the moment is to build on what you have managed to achieve and to find ways to make certain that your present confidence is well founded.

13 THURSDAY · Moon Age Day 22 · Moon Sign Taurus

Venus remains in your solar twelfth house, indicating a feeling of being somewhat cut off emotionally. Even if the path towards your objectives is clear and easy to follow in almost every other way, there may be something inside you that demands more, especially in terms of relationships. It is possible that you are expecting too much.

14 FRIDAY · Moon Age Day 23 · Moon Sign Taurus

There is much to be said for sticking to the point in your dealings with others, so that there is no chance of misinterpretation or confusion. By all means give yourself a pat on the back for anything that has gone your way this week, but beware of taking your eye off the ball. It's worth being prepared to deal with some opposition.

♌

15 SATURDAY   *Moon Age Day 24   Moon Sign Gemini*

At this time you can afford to display your individualism in almost everything you do. This could reflect in the way you choose to dress and also in terms of your unconventional view of everyday matters. Some people might even accuse you of being eccentric this month, but that shouldn't bother you in the least.

16 SUNDAY   *Moon Age Day 25   Moon Sign Gemini*

Even if there is a great deal going on in your social life, trends also encourage you to show your love and regard for that someone special in your life. Friendships shine out strongly, and you might even decide to put yourself back in the warm embrace of someone who disappeared from your life for ages.

17 MONDAY   *Moon Age Day 26   Moon Sign Cancer*

The Moon in your twelfth house generally denotes a period of self-control and a need for solitude. This is an ideal time for getting involved with serious matters from the past, or planning very carefully for the future. You might wish to ignore the world today but it probably isn't going to leave you alone!

18 TUESDAY   *Moon Age Day 27   Moon Sign Cancer*

The focus is still on getting to grips with important matters, though you now have scope to discover ways and means to move forward without putting in quite so much effort. After all, the Sun is still strong in your zodiac sign, enhancing your optimism but also your effectiveness. Friends could well have good news.

19 WEDNESDAY   *Moon Age Day 28   Moon Sign Leo*

The lunar high offers an opportunity to be on top, and it would take someone very competent and extremely clever to get ahead of you in the power stakes. Despite the fact that your dominant side is emphasised, you can still help those around you – but of course you expect them to show how very grateful they are.

20 THURSDAY
Moon Age Day 0   Moon Sign Leo

You have scope to make this one of the best times of the year for fresh starts and for getting your head around problems that have beset you for a while. It's worth concentrating your energy in specific directions and showing the world just how capable Leo can be. At the same time you you needn't hide your affections.

21 FRIDAY
Moon Age Day 1   Moon Sign Virgo

It looks as though your love life may be your least source of pleasure during this twenty-four-hour period – though there appears to be no hard reason for this state of affairs. It's all down to the present position of Venus, which supports some restlessness and an inability to express your emotions as easily as you normally can.

22 SATURDAY
Moon Age Day 2   Moon Sign Virgo

Little Mercury has now moved on in your chart and offers the chance for you to achieve a greater sense of security in money matters. You are entering a period that will be ideal for all business transactions, and even if you don't think this can have a bearing on your life, it will. Purchases made now should be considered and wise.

23 SUNDAY
Moon Age Day 3   Moon Sign Libra

Now the Sun joins Mercury in your second house, and financial prospects take a turn for the better. Be prepared to find out where the bargains are, and to leap in and make a killing before others are even alert to situations. A day to use your quick-witted and funny nature to make a great impression.

24 MONDAY
Moon Age Day 4   Moon Sign Libra

If you are unsure regarding a specific plan of action, it might help if you enlist the support of people who are really in the know. The same is generally true when it comes to jobs that need doing around the house. You could struggle yourself, but in the end it will probably prove to be cheaper and easier to get someone in.

25 TUESDAY *Moon Age Day 5 Moon Sign Scorpio*

Your general behaviour today tends to be influenced by a sort of 'other-worldly' attitude and by the strongest intuitions imaginable. That little voice inside your head that tells you what to do, and when to do it, should not be ignored. You can even use it to help you get on better at work and to make sensible financial decisions.

26 WEDNESDAY *Moon Age Day 6 Moon Sign Scorpio*

Your strength lies in your inventive, quick mind, which you can use to race ahead of others in almost all situations. That's fine, except that they may not understand your actions or even the reasoning behind them. It would help today if you were willing to explain yourself and even to spell things out in very specific terms.

27 THURSDAY *Moon Age Day 7 Moon Sign Scorpio*

Venus now stands strongly in your solar first house. This assists you to handle your love life and to put yourself in touch with some interesting new people. Another positive result of this planetary position is that you can increase your popularity and persuade others to do anything for you.

28 FRIDAY *Moon Age Day 8 Moon Sign Sagittarius*

The time is right to make sure you are both spontaneous and fascinating to know, and to do all you can to make those around you as happy as possible. There are gains to be made by getting out and about with individuals who feed your intellect and who seem to think about things just as you do.

29 SATURDAY *Moon Age Day 9 Moon Sign Sagittarius*

Even if it isn't possible to get on equally well with everyone today, that may be as much due to their attitudes as to your own. Your best approach is to stay away from anyone you find difficult. It would be far better today to spend as much time as you can in the company of people you have known for a very long time.

30 SUNDAY   *Moon Age Day 10   Moon Sign Capricorn*

The things that are happening to you but which are not planned by you could turn out to be the most important issues of all today. True, you might not feel as though you are fully in control, but that shouldn't matter too much if the end product turns out to be positive. The evening offers an ideal chance for personal grooming and luxury.

31 MONDAY   *Moon Age Day 11   Moon Sign Capricorn*

Social settings are well accented today, even though you might also be putting a lot of effort into your work. It seems that you get on better when you are not really trying, and there may be an object lesson here. There is a possibility that you are trying too hard in some spheres of your life. Don't be afraid to relax and enjoy the ride.

September
2009

1 TUESDAY
Moon Age Day 12   Moon Sign Capricorn

The first day of September has potential to be generally positive, particularly if you show a gregarious face to the world and remain determined to keep everyone laughing. Creative potential is highlighted, and this could be the best time of all for making changes at home that will keep you comfortable in the months ahead.

2 WEDNESDAY
Moon Age Day 13   Moon Sign Aquarius

If certain issues seem to be out of control, you can thank the arrival of the lunar low. Take heart though, because when things do go wrong you have scope to see the humour in the situation. There is much to be said for discovering just how funny and rewarding the odd failure can be now.

3 THURSDAY
Moon Age Day 14   Moon Sign Aquarius

Self-expression could be slightly inhibited today, and even if this isn't a major problem, you may be left with the feeling that you haven't said at all what you intended. It's worth making time to put things right later. In the meantime, today responds best if you take some rest and just watch for a while.

4 FRIDAY
Moon Age Day 15   Moon Sign Pisces

As September gains pace, trends support a break from your normal routines and a general sense of restlessness. There is great potential for travel, even if you hadn't really thought about doing so at this time. Be prepared to lend support to people who rely on you, since letting them down isn't an option.

5 SATURDAY   *Moon Age Day 16   Moon Sign Pisces*

Along comes an influence that has a strong bearing on both friendships and your love life. Your personal magnetism is enhanced, and you shouldn't have any trouble at all attracting the right people to help you along. In every way you have what it takes to display yourself to the world as a true son or daughter of Leo should.

6 SUNDAY   *Moon Age Day 17   Moon Sign Pisces*

Your desire for greater freedom of self-expression encourages you to take any opportunity to tell others what you think. Your opinions might not always be welcome, but in the main you can retain your popularity and esteem. Today works best if you find something new and different to do.

7 MONDAY   ☿   *Moon Age Day 18   Moon Sign Aries*

Generally speaking this ought to be a great time for wheeling and dealing. It's worth doing all the business you can this week and capitalising on the positive trends that surround you on all sides. It's time to get busy, and you can persuade plenty of people in your vicinity to throw in their lot with you.

8 TUESDAY   ☿   *Moon Age Day 19   Moon Sign Aries*

Today offers a chance to deal positively with a past issue and also put your personal life into a better focus. If arguments have occurred, now is the time to do everything you can to put an end to them. Nevertheless, yours is a very reactive zodiac sign and you can't expect to agree with everyone all of the time.

9 WEDNESDAY   ☿   *Moon Age Day 20   Moon Sign Taurus*

Mercury in your third house offers a mental peak and a time when things seem so clear-cut that you can't understand why you didn't deal with them efficiently before. Logic is also highlighted, and you have scope to consider many factors in the decisions you make now. You can maintain your popularity in social situations.

10 THURSDAY ☿ *Moon Age Day 21* *Moon Sign Taurus*

Today you can make the most of a magnetic quality that allows you to attract people to you. Part of the reason why things should be going well is that Venus is still in your first house. This enhances your loving and loveable nature and assists you to express your affection and even your passion to a much greater extent.

11 FRIDAY ☿ *Moon Age Day 22* *Moon Sign Gemini*

By all means do what you can to stimulate new and fascinating attachments, but at the same time it's worth ensuring that these don't interfere with your most intimate relationships. A little jealousy is possible under present trends, and even if this is without justification, it may be understandable.

12 SATURDAY ☿ *Moon Age Day 23* *Moon Sign Gemini*

If you want to get the very best of what is on offer this weekend, your best approach is to be disciplined. There may be a slight tendency for you to let certain things ride, or to expect others to take up the slack. There are some decisions that only you can make, and if you leave them to those around you, the results could be chaotic.

13 SUNDAY ☿ *Moon Age Day 24* *Moon Sign Cancer*

Your mind remains good, and you have what it takes to let others know what everyone ought to be doing. Don't be too surprised if someone has ideas of their own and refuses to follow your advice. If you remain flexible and open-minded you can avoid your perfect model of life being shattered at a stroke.

14 MONDAY ☿ *Moon Age Day 25* *Moon Sign Cancer*

Trends heighten your desire to get things done at the start of this week, as well as your ability to find the necessary components. Even if there are occasions when you are thwarted by the different notions of colleagues or friends, in the main you can get life to go your way and can impress the most important people.

15 TUESDAY ☿ *Moon Age Day 26 Moon Sign Leo*

The lunar high this month favours change and personal growth. This is a very good time to push forward towards major goals and objectives, without allowing others to stand in your way. Professional relationships are well accented, and no matter what you are doing, your strength lies in making a good impression.

16 WEDNESDAY ☿ *Moon Age Day 27 Moon Sign Leo*

Energy reaches a peak and you might have capacity to spare today. You can use your potential for success in every area of your life, and it may seem as though you simply can't stop moving. Wednesday might not be the best time for going to a dance, but that could well be the best place for your itchy feet!

17 THURSDAY ☿ *Moon Age Day 28 Moon Sign Virgo*

Perhaps thankfully you can afford to be a little more sedate in your thoughts and actions now that the lunar high is over. Now is the time to show your easy-going nature to the full and to get out into some wide-open spaces along with people you care for. A deeper and more spiritual side of your nature is to the fore today.

18 FRIDAY ☿ *Moon Age Day 29 Moon Sign Virgo*

You would be wise to listen to the advice of people in your vicinity today, especially in the case of those individuals for whom you have the greatest respect. Making up your own mind about everything is fine, but you might not be fully in the know. This is a period when it would be best to gather together all the information you can.

19 SATURDAY ☿ *Moon Age Day 0 Moon Sign Virgo*

Your communication skills are still enhanced, as is your ability to make financial progress. That doesn't mean putting your shirt on the next horse running, but it can be useful in matters of business. Why not get in touch with people you don't see too often, by whatever means you have at your disposal?

20 SUNDAY   ☿   *Moon Age Day 1   Moon Sign Libra*

Venus has now moved from your first to your solar second house, and this can be very helpful from a financial point of view. True, you might find personal attachments slightly more difficult to deal with than you did last week, but your charm puts you in a position to bring people round, even if they are difficult at first.

21 MONDAY   ☿   *Moon Age Day 2   Moon Sign Libra*

There are trends around at the moment that encourage you to look back rather than forward. Leo is going through a nostalgic phase, and it is possible that elements of your past will replay in your mind a great deal this week. This needn't be a problem as long as you remember that for a Leo things can only really happen in the present.

22 TUESDAY   ☿   *Moon Age Day 3   Moon Sign Scorpio*

Venus continues to offer a boost in financial affairs. This can be small, but should gain strength in the days to come. It would be wise to put yourself in the best possible position when making deals, primarily by knowing what you are talking about. If you don't, there may well be people around who would be happy to advise you.

23 WEDNESDAY ☿   *Moon Age Day 4   Moon Sign Scorpio*

A strong boost to finances is still indicated – that is if you put yourself in the best position to benefit from these positive trends. That will mean keeping your eyes open and acting quickly when you know the time is right. New and valuable information is there for the taking, so make sure you don't ignore it.

24 THURSDAY   ☿ *Moon Age Day 5   Moon Sign Sagittarius*

Getting your own way at home could cause some conflict, but you might find it hard to back down from your chosen position right now. There are compromises to be had, but finding them may not be at all easy. You may decide that people you don't see on a regular basis are the best ones to spend time with at this stage.

25 FRIDAY ☿ *Moon Age Day 6   Moon Sign Sagittarius*

Love life and romantic matters generally count for a great deal today. A slightly less contentious approach is possible, and it's worth choosing a version of the truth that others find easier to stomach. If you engage others rather than dominating them, that might be all it takes to persuade them to do things your way.

26 SATURDAY ☿ *Moon Age Day 7   Moon Sign Capricorn*

You can still use your good communication skills to persuade others that you know what you are talking about, but the emphasis today is much more on social matters than it will be on business. Be prepared to contribute to team games or any situation in which you are part of a group and not flying solo.

27 SUNDAY ☿ *Moon Age Day 8   Moon Sign Capricorn*

Certain matters in your personal life could be either misleading or confused today, and it might be worth talking things through carefully in order to discover what is really going on. There are a few snags about and a little more care will be necessary when you are trying to understand what makes younger family members tick.

28 MONDAY ☿ *Moon Age Day 9   Moon Sign Capricorn*

Progress could well be too slow for your liking, especially later on today. This is because the Moon is moving back into Aquarius, from where it does you few favours. Be prepared to deal with possible confusion about matters you thought you understood only too well, and keep your thought processes in order.

29 TUESDAY ☿ *Moon Age Day 10   Moon Sign Aquarius*

There could be minor tensions about today, and even if these mean little individually, when lumped together frustration could well be the result. Why not withdraw somewhat from the rat race and spend a few hours on your own, if not during the day, perhaps this evening? It's hard to fall out with yourself!

30 WEDNESDAY ☿ *Moon Age Day 11   Moon Sign Aquarius*

Rather than expecting too many favours from life at the moment, your best approach is to plug on in your own sweet way. There could well be struggles around, but these will only have a bearing on your life if you choose to become involved. Needless to say, important matters are best put on hold, but most likely only until tomorrow.

October

2009

1 THURSDAY
Moon Age Day 12   Moon Sign Pisces

Things are on the up again and what looked confusing or problematic yesterday now comes into sharp relief. Once you identify potential stumbling blocks you are well able to deal with them, and as a result can clear the path before you. Your usual cheerful nature will also be a distinct advantage in social settings today.

2 FRIDAY
Moon Age Day 13   Moon Sign Pisces

Venus remains in your solar second house. From here it is perfectly placed to help you at work and especially when it comes to bringing positive emotion to bear on practical situations. Persuading others that you are the best person for any job ought to be a piece of cake, particularly if you use your magnetism to the full.

3 SATURDAY
Moon Age Day 14   Moon Sign Pisces

An ideal time to turn your interests towards cultural matters and to mix with people or associations that have not played a part in your life up to now. Trends also enhance the charitable side of your nature, and you have scope to find ways to help out those who you see as being far less fortunate than you are.

4 SUNDAY
Moon Age Day 15   Moon Sign Aries

Mars remains in your solar twelfth house, where it has now been for quite some time. This provides certain undertones to life and can lead to the feeling that you are being manipulated in some way. The problem comes not from any paranoia that results from this, but from those occasions when it turns out to be true.

5 MONDAY
Moon Age Day 16   Moon Sign Aries

You should bring out your mental gifts now and use them for all you are worth. Halfway between intuitional and inspirational, you can make almost anything go your way. You have what it takes to deal with several tasks at the same time, and you shouldn't be easily thwarted by the odd setback that might occur.

6 TUESDAY
Moon Age Day 17   Moon Sign Taurus

The Sun is now in your solar third house, encouraging a chattier approach for much of this month. The time is right to show what you have to say for yourself in most circumstances, and to use your persuasive powers to bring others round to your point of view. Romantic relationships are very well starred now.

7 WEDNESDAY
Moon Age Day 18   Moon Sign Taurus

Mars still occupies its position, brooding over your life at a distance and sometimes taking the edge off your successes. If difficulties do arise you can afford to go with the flow more and to rely on the good offices of colleagues and friends. Be ready to make the most of good news on the financial front any day now.

8 THURSDAY
Moon Age Day 19   Moon Sign Gemini

Positive influences surround social encounters, and you have scope to make progress though your dealings with different groups and organisations. When you tire of one thing, don't be afraid to move onto another. It's worth using your ingenuity to the full when dealing with minor panics.

9 FRIDAY
Moon Age Day 20   Moon Sign Gemini

The position of the Sun makes this period mentally inspirational and very exciting. Many of the gains and benefits that are available now come like a bolt from the blue and it is important to stand ready to make your move at almost any time. Away from work, you can afford to relax and make the most of family moments.

10 SATURDAY   *Moon Age Day 21   Moon Sign Gemini*

As the Moon moves into your solar twelfth house you enter a slightly quieter period – a time when the closer and more personal aspects of life come under greater scrutiny. Much of your planning today is best done behind closed doors, away from the prying eyes of anyone you see as being either naturally nosy or downright interfering.

11 SUNDAY   *Moon Age Day 22   Moon Sign Cancer*

If you need to get some vital message across to others, now is the time to go for it, whilst Mercury is in such a good position. It shares the same house in your solar chart as the Sun, and that enhances not only your incentive to speak your mind but also the means to do so. Beware of getting caught up with minor details at home.

12 MONDAY   *Moon Age Day 23   Moon Sign Cancer*

This is the final day before the lunar high for October begins to have a tangible part to play in your life. You would be wise to steady down somewhat and decide exactly what you want at the moment. This is worthwhile because there is good fortune on offer, plus the chance for you to use your skills to the very best of your ability.

13 TUESDAY   *Moon Age Day 24   Moon Sign Leo*

This is a time to get ahead by jumping the queue. If you make use of your charms, others shouldn't worry too much that you are not waiting around to be asked, and in any case this is not the way Leo acts when working at its best. In addition to your silver tongue, you can also draw on tremendous intuition, a gift without parallel.

14 WEDNESDAY   *Moon Age Day 25   Moon Sign Leo*

You have scope to make this a high point in terms of your general plans, and it's worth using every skill in your armoury to get where you want to be. If this means gently nudging others out of the way, so be it. You can worry about helping them once you are where you rightfully belong. You can't be too sensitive today.

15 THURSDAY   *Moon Age Day 26   Moon Sign Virgo*

The Sun offers a period of comings and goings – though it has to be said that this is probably the way you want things to be at present. Although you are generally solid in your affections and as steadfast as anyone, for a while a more flexible and slightly less fixed approach works best. An ideal day to ask for a favour.

16 FRIDAY   *Moon Age Day 27   Moon Sign Virgo*

Once again you can demonstrate a tremendous talent for being persuasive, even in situations that would have colleagues or friends baffled. Your strength lies in getting people to follow your lead, and in showing them that 'winner' is written through you like a stick of rock.

17 SATURDAY   *Moon Age Day 28   Moon Sign Libra*

At long last Mars has moved out of your twelfth house and into your first, which puts it in your own zodiac sign of Leo. This is a noteworthy event because it removes a number of barriers and enhances your individuality. At the same time you can afford to act on wider impulses without worrying about the consequences.

18 SUNDAY   *Moon Age Day 0   Moon Sign Libra*

Mental restlessness could, and indeed should, incline you to abandon tradition ways of getting things done in favour of seeking out new ideas or situations. It's all about stimulation under present trends, and you now have scope to achieve payback for all the effort you have put into life. A day to show your exotic and intriguing side.

19 MONDAY   *Moon Age Day 1   Moon Sign Scorpio*

A domestic matter could prove tiresome in some way, particularly if there is much you want to do out there in the wider world. If feelings are coming to the surface, that could mean serious talks, though you may not really want this at the moment. Nevertheless, it's worth taking the time out to try and understand.

20 TUESDAY
Moon Age Day 2   Moon Sign Scorpio

For the moment the Sun remains in the third house of your chart, offering a definite intellectual boost to your nature. It supports a fondness for good literature or for the sort of conversation that is deep and even spiritual in content. There can be something of the philosopher about you now, which isn't that odd for a Leo.

21 WEDNESDAY
Moon Age Day 3   Moon Sign Sagittarius

This might turn out to be the best time of the month to make yourself the centre of attention. If people are pleased to have you around, it should be easy for you to find the right words to impress anyone at all. You might be especially good at impressing superiors, and can use your skills to capitalise on an intriguing offer.

22 THURSDAY
Moon Age Day 4   Moon Sign Sagittarius

Now that Mars has finally entered your first house, you can show the world a more outgoing and even perhaps a little more aggressive approach than of late. You can demonstrate this in a number of different ways, and can exploit the planetary position for any work-based matter. Beware of biting off more than you can chew.

23 FRIDAY
Moon Age Day 5   Moon Sign Sagittarius

The time is right to look again at a recent project at work and to bring a little more ingenuity to bear on it than you did before. If normal responses don't work in affairs of the heart, you may decide to try a slightly more ingenious approach. It's worth paying attention to all the small details of life.

24 SATURDAY
Moon Age Day 6   Moon Sign Capricorn

A great sense of togetherness is possible, and this is emphasised by the fact that the Sun has now moved into your solar fourth house. For the next three or four weeks trends encourage a greater focus on home and family than is usually the case, and you can afford to do as much as possible to make relatives feel good.

25 SUNDAY   *Moon Age Day 7   Moon Sign Capricorn*

Mercury now sharpens your social and conversational skills, assisting you to become an avid debater about anything and everything. There are some things in which you need to give way to those who are older or wiser than you are, but in the main you should be able to get onto the right side of more or less anyone.

26 MONDAY   *Moon Age Day 8   Moon Sign Aquarius*

Beware a tendency towards impulsive behaviour whilst the lunar low is around. Even if you start out positively enough, there are times today and tomorrow when running out of steam is a distinct possibility. Obligations could get in the way, and yet they might at the same time be the source of some comfort.

27 TUESDAY   *Moon Age Day 9   Moon Sign Aquarius*

You may now decide to rely on the help you can obtain from others. Actually there is nothing at all wrong with this. If you spend a great part of your life assisting anyone and everyone, why shouldn't you get something in return? It's probable that you like to feel that you are always in command, which of course is not true!

28 WEDNESDAY   *Moon Age Day 10   Moon Sign Aquarius*

Though Mars now enhances your energy, confidence and vigour there are times when you need to be careful that you are not going just a little too far. You need to consider the feelings of other people and make sure you are not riding roughshod over their sensibilities. Even if that isn't a problem now, it could be one later.

29 THURSDAY   *Moon Age Day 11   Moon Sign Pisces*

Family life has potential to bring out the best in you whilst the Sun occupies your fourth house. Home can be a source of extended entertainment, and you may already be planning for an 'at home' sort of weekend to come. As the days get colder your fireside seems more welcoming, but your social instincts remain strong.

30 FRIDAY
Moon Age Day 12   Moon Sign Pisces

A continuing commitment to home and family may be a reflection of what is happening to those you love. Perhaps there are new incentives for younger people, or an improvement in the health of someone who has been out of sorts. Trends indicate a desire to involve yourself in gossip today, which is not all that odd.

31 SATURDAY
Moon Age Day 13   Moon Sign Aries

If your mind is working fast, you may show a tendency to express yourself in a hurried manner. Under present influences, no sooner do you arrive than you are on the move again, and your actions might make those around you slightly dizzy. An ideal day to think deeply about a link with the past.

November
2009

1 SUNDAY
Moon Age Day 14   Moon Sign Aries

This is another marvellous time to get out into the social world – or even to attract it to your own door. You have scope to make new contacts and to capitalise on a number of fascinating possibilities that are on offer. Prepare now to make the most of positive changes once the new week gets underway.

2 MONDAY
Moon Age Day 15   Moon Sign Aries

This is a time when you can happily put yourself in the limelight and enjoy all the accolades that are coming your way. If you make sure what you are doing involves subjects you understand only too well, you can maintain your confidence. On the rare occasions that you come unstuck in conversations, try to see the funny side!

3 TUESDAY
Moon Age Day 16   Moon Sign Taurus

What you need at this stage of the week are as many different interests as proves to be possible. By all means cherry pick until you find what suits you the best, and then in a day or two you can concentrate more on specifics. For the moment it's worth letting your mind wander freely without being restricted in anything at all.

4 WEDNESDAY
Moon Age Day 17   Moon Sign Taurus

This is an especially good time to be working in groups or with individuals you get on with. Even if colleagues are demanding, bear in mind that they ask as much of themselves as they do of you, and that makes all the difference. You can't do enough at the moment for someone you really like, and that could be just about everyone.

5 THURSDAY
Moon Age Day 18   Moon Sign Gemini

Trends support a sense of optimism and a thirst for new ideas in practically everything you are doing at this stage of the month. Being pleasant to others enables you to gain affection in return, plus the chance of a great deal of practical help too. There may be so many people queuing up to do you favours that it could be embarrassing.

6 FRIDAY
Moon Age Day 19   Moon Sign Gemini

Don't be afraid to take plenty of time to make up your mind about personal matters, rather than making any precipitous decisions for the moment. You have scope to let things ride and allow yourself more room to look at the broader possibilities of life. Sooner or later you will have to make choices, but preferably not today or tomorrow.

7 SATURDAY
Moon Age Day 20   Moon Sign Cancer

With Mars in your solar first house you should be quite ready to take on the work in all practical matters and to make the most of opportunities to do so. Finding excitement in almost anything is about being in a state of expectation and readiness. Even if not everyone is helpful, you can persuade most people to be so.

8 SUNDAY
Moon Age Day 21   Moon Sign Cancer

By tomorrow the Moon will be back in your sign, but today responds best if you retire into yourself more than has been the case for much of this week. Your fireside may be welcoming, and yet underneath your quieter exterior there is a burning desire to get out there and do things. Try to curb your impatience, until tomorrow at least.

9 MONDAY
Moon Age Day 22   Moon Sign Leo

Now you get the chance to take the initiative and to demonstrate how good your ideas really are. The lunar high coincides with the start of a new week, and assists you to excel in practical and professional matters. Good fortune is on your side, so you can afford to push your luck a lot more than you usually might.

10 TUESDAY   *Moon Age Day 23   Moon Sign Leo*

You have what it takes to turn even failure into sparkling success right now, though you need to focus all your attention in specific directions if you are to really show your worth. There is great warmth on offer at the moment, though probably not from the weather! A day to light up everyone's world with your cheery smile.

11 WEDNESDAY   *Moon Age Day 24   Moon Sign Virgo*

With the Sun snuggled down in your solar fourth house you are encouraged to seek comfort and luxury for the next week or two. Whether you will actually find either remains in some slight doubt, because on the other hand there are planetary trends that push you onward and insist that you travel light and fast.

12 THURSDAY   *Moon Age Day 25   Moon Sign Virgo*

Even if domestic matters turn out very much in the way you would wish, there could still be something niggling away at the back of your mind. Perhaps you have worries about a relative or you could think that you have inadvertently upset someone? Either way, you need to consider whether you are overplaying the situation.

13 FRIDAY   *Moon Age Day 26   Moon Sign Libra*

Friday the thirteenth should find you happily on the go and not the least worried about the traditions of this particular day. You can turn most situations to your advantage, and when you turn on that smile you shouldn't have to work too hard to enlist support. In group situations you can be first amongst equals at the moment.

14 SATURDAY   *Moon Age Day 27   Moon Sign Libra*

With Mars in such a strong position this is a good time to lead in any project, whether it involves your work or social life. If you know how to make others laugh, that can prove to be a distinct advantage this weekend. Beware of reacting too harshly to offhand comments. They probably aren't worth the effort.

15 SUNDAY   *Moon Age Day 28   Moon Sign Scorpio*

A slightly nostalgic mood could prevail today, and there is much to be said for taking a less demanding role for a few hours. Wallowing in the past is not usually your thing, but for once it might bring out the best in you. You can also learn valuable lessons, and perhaps find laughter, in the things you did once upon a time.

16 MONDAY   *Moon Age Day 29   Moon Sign Scorpio*

Even if home is where you would prefer to be today, instead you may be thrust out into an unsuspecting world. All sorts of family matters can benefit from your wisdom and common sense if you are able to curl up by your own fireside, whereas more practical matters could seem awkward and difficult today, thanks to the Moon.

17 TUESDAY   *Moon Age Day 0   Moon Sign Scorpio*

The Moon has less of a bearing on your life today and Mars will predominate as a result. This allows you to be buoyed up by confidence and to show a real zest for life in all its flavours. New possibilities are on the way, and you could even now be looking towards plans that will mature by early next year.

18 WEDNESDAY   *Moon Age Day 1   Moon Sign Sagittarius*

Positive highlights appear beneath social and leisure interests. Your popularity is potentially at a peak and your impressive personality can be a definite boon. At work you have what it takes to show colleagues and superiors alike how efficient the zodiac sign of Leo can be. Don't be afraid to attract attention to your actions.

19 THURSDAY   *Moon Age Day 2   Moon Sign Sagittarius*

Make the most of an extremely creative period and one that offers much in the way of inventiveness. Solving puzzles is just one of your skills under present trends, and it doesn't really matter whether these are leisure matters or associated with life itself. Your company is welcome almost anywhere, particularly if you remain adaptable.

20 FRIDAY   *Moon Age Day 3   Moon Sign Capricorn*

Beware of rushing ahead too much with practical decisions just now. There are definite options around, and it's worth looking at all of them before you make up your mind about almost anything. This runs contrary to the usual Leo way of proceeding, because you are generally inclined to act or react extremely quickly.

21 SATURDAY   *Moon Age Day 4   Moon Sign Capricorn*

Daily affairs could be more enjoyable now due to pleasant domestic influences, especially if loved ones have your best interests at heart. All of this helps you to make this a pleasant sort of Saturday, but one that also demands a certain amount of effort on your part. What a great day this would be for a trip to town. Shopping calls!

22 SUNDAY   *Moon Age Day 5   Moon Sign Capricorn*

This Sunday remains a time of opportunity, and there are solid reasons for taking the lead in all group and social matters. Your love life should also be coming up to scratch, partly because you can be attentive and caring. Tomorrow brings less flexibility and a more isolated quality, but for now you should be on form.

23 MONDAY   *Moon Age Day 6   Moon Sign Aquarius*

The lunar low could slow you down considerably this time around, but this is not something you should be worrying about to any great extent. Your best approach is to let life flow by and allow those around you to row the boat for a change. Rather than expecting a lucky break, why not keep your demands reasonable?

24 TUESDAY   *Moon Age Day 7   Moon Sign Aquarius*

A day to exercise caution in business matters and avoid spending large amounts of money unless you are positive that everything has been sorted out as much as is possible. You may not find many bargains around whilst the Moon is in Aquarius, so the advice is that you should keep your options open for another day.

25 WEDNESDAY   *Moon Age Day 8   Moon Sign Pisces*

While you were busy doing other things, the Sun has moved on in your chart and it now occupies your solar fifth house. From this position it offers a boost to your ego, assisting you to get yourself noticed. Although you may not realise the fact, in a moment-by-moment sense it is important for you to maintain your popularity.

26 THURSDAY   *Moon Age Day 9   Moon Sign Pisces*

Your forte right now is to make a comfortable home environment and to enjoy the quieter and less strenuous possibilities that come along during the winter months. Not that you necessarily enjoy this time of year very much. Leo is a creature of the Sun, and any opportunity to feel its warmth somewhere else should be seriously considered.

27 FRIDAY   *Moon Age Day 10   Moon Sign Pisces*

Mars positively insists that you take command today, even if colleagues or friends seem unwilling to relinquish control. If you do leave everything to others, difficulties are possible in certain aspects of your life. The problem is that nobody but you has the winning formula that is really needed at present.

28 SATURDAY   *Moon Age Day 11   Moon Sign Aries*

What a great day this would be for romance and for showing your partner just how important they are to you. If you are between relationships at the moment, now is one of the best times to concentrate your efforts and to impress someone who could become quite special. Be careful you don't overindulge in anything.

29 SUNDAY   *Moon Age Day 12   Moon Sign Aries*

The time is right to take full advantage of emotional links with friends and family, and also to plan with others how the Christmas period is going to be handled. Someone extremely close to you could be a great help without even realising the fact, and you would be wise to make the most of opportunities to prove how faithful you are.

30 MONDAY   *Moon Age Day 13   Moon Sign Taurus*

A more adventurous state of mind is inspired by an ever-strengthening Mars. Certainly this is an excellent time for new ambitions, though it is important to check all facts carefully before you embark on anything remotely risky. Be prepared to seek advice from people who genuinely do know better.

December
2009

1 TUESDAY
Moon Age Day 14   Moon Sign Taurus

Your strengths lie in career-related matters on the first day of December. Trends encourage you to be diligent and ambitious, and to show just how considered your actions are. Some Leos may now be pursuing advancement, and if you are one of them it's worth starting a new regime in the way you intend to carry it on.

2 WEDNESDAY
Moon Age Day 15   Moon Sign Gemini

Set the precedent for a good day by making an early start. The more you get done first thing, the greater can be your success later in the day. You needn't let people or situations stand in your way at this time, and that first-house Mars keeps urging you on. By the evening you may well be more than ready to put your feet up!

3 THURSDAY
Moon Age Day 16   Moon Sign Gemini

The present position of the Moon makes today especially good for working in large groups or for getting to grips with matters that involve a large number of individuals. Anything that gets you noticed has to be good, and what is really important about this time is how well you can shine out in company. This builds greater confidence.

4 FRIDAY
Moon Age Day 17   Moon Sign Cancer

A day to be yourself, without any frills and fancies. No matter how well you dress or what car you drive, what really matters is your personality. Having said that, don't be afraid to spice up your romantic life with some grandiose gestures, and if you can find the time, you can afford to put on an extra display of love.

5 SATURDAY

Moon Age Day 18   Moon Sign Cancer

If energy levels are slightly low ahead of the lunar high, you may well decide to take some time to yourself today. This could involve a later start than usual or a desire to lounge around the house for at least part of the day. By the afternoon the Moon is moving on, and you have a chance to think about a more social sort of evening.

6 SUNDAY

Moon Age Day 19   Moon Sign Leo

It is your job now to pave the way to the future, with new ideas and a bolder approach. December has already arrived, and you need to consider whether there are still ambitions for this year that have not been realised. There are three weeks left, and the lunar high offers you all the incentive you need to make that final, decisive push.

7 MONDAY

Moon Age Day 20   Moon Sign Leo

It seems as though almost anything is possible today, and with plenty of energy and incentive on your part you have what you need to make a good impression. At work you can leave all competition far behind, and when it comes to your social life you can be at the forefront of all activity. Potentially one of the best days of the month.

8 TUESDAY

Moon Age Day 21   Moon Sign Virgo

Romantic relationships are in the spotlight, and this is also a perfect day for checking out the most exciting social events and for signing yourself up to them. The time is right to get yourself noticed, and you shouldn't let an opportunity pass you by. The only slight downside is if there are any awkward types about.

9 WEDNESDAY

Moon Age Day 22   Moon Sign Virgo

Another day to focus your sights on love and romance. This is where a good deal of the joy resides under present trends, and with December comes a certain warmth that isn't possible at other times of year. Think carefully about changing well-laid Christmas plans – remember that they involve other people as well as you!

10 THURSDAY · Moon Age Day 23 · Moon Sign Libra

Be prepared to further plans and objectives with new information that you can discover around this time. You can afford to be particularly chatty right now and to listen to what others have to say. Being nosey can sometimes work out to your distinct advantage, but it doesn't do anything for that noble Leo persona.

11 FRIDAY · Moon Age Day 24 · Moon Sign Libra

With a king-sized ego at the moment, this is the time to strike out on your own and to make it plain to an unsuspecting world that you really are king of the jungle! Capitalising on your heightened energy may be difficult if you find that the special needs of December are getting in your way. Never mind, you can be festive later.

12 SATURDAY · Moon Age Day 25 · Moon Sign Libra

Trends support a strong wish to make your domestic surroundings just as comfortable as can be. Loved ones might have a great deal to contribute and you shouldn't belittle their contributions, even accidentally. A day to think before you speak, and to make sure that you give appropriate praise where it is due.

13 SUNDAY · Moon Age Day 26 · Moon Sign Scorpio

Along comes a potential high spot for those of you who work on a Sunday. If you toil away in the retail trade you might be especially busy at the moment, but that needn't worry you if your energy levels are quite high. Leos who can relax today may decide not to do so at all. Be prepared for some bargain-hunting!

14 MONDAY · Moon Age Day 27 · Moon Sign Scorpio

Today offers you a chance to fulfil your desire for romance. This trend assists you to renew and invigorate relationships and to whisper those special words that mean so much to your partner or sweetheart. Those Leos who don't have someone special in their lives at present would be wise to look towards new possibilities.

15 TUESDAY   *Moon Age Day 28   Moon Sign Sagittarius*

Once again you can make the most of an increase in all pleasurable endeavours. Now is the time to use your present energy to enjoy life to the full. New and better possibilities at work might be on offer, and these may be a result of someone else's slightly bad luck, though you shouldn't blame yourself for that eventuality.

16 WEDNESDAY   *Moon Age Day 0   Moon Sign Sagittarius*

The Sun in your solar fifth house has the power to bring out the best qualities of Leo. Your romantic side is still stimulated and your powers of attraction should be much increased as a result. Typical of your nature at its best, you can afford to be generous with your affections, and that helps you to gain plenty of admirers.

17 THURSDAY   *Moon Age Day 1   Moon Sign Capricorn*

Minor plans can start to bear real fruit, enabling you to make gains you may not have expected. For one thing, you have scope to improve your financial situation, though at the same time you probably won't have any problem spending money. Your main concern today should be perceptive planning for the way ahead.

18 FRIDAY   *Moon Age Day 2   Moon Sign Capricorn*

With Mars in your first house and the Sun still in your fifth, your ego reaches a peak, assisting you to assume personal leadership in all sorts of situations. Unlike most people, for whom power tends to corrupt, it doesn't do so in your case. You have a chance to show the best and most noble side of your nature as you forge ahead.

19 SATURDAY   *Moon Age Day 3   Moon Sign Capricorn*

Today marks something of a watershed for you, because by tomorrow the lunar low is around and after that the Sun moves on into your sixth house. If there is any unfinished business to be done, it's worth getting it out of the way now. Your desires are likely to alter somewhat, and the demands of Christmas will be upon you.

20 SUNDAY   *Moon Age Day 4   Moon Sign Aquarius*

Rather than expecting to get too much done today, be willing to rest and relax as much as possible. This is the best way of avoiding any fractiousness with yourself if you can't find things and if life seems a little upset by all the comings and goings. This is a short period of indecision and anxiety, caused by the lunar low.

21 MONDAY   *Moon Age Day 5   Moon Sign Aquarius*

It might seem that you are suddenly totally lacking in ambition. Because you are a child of the moment, what you feel today will appear to be forever, though of course it is only very temporary. All of a sudden you won't be ready for Christmas, and panic could be the result. Never mind, by the evening you should be back to normal.

22 TUESDAY   *Moon Age Day 6   Moon Sign Pisces*

It's time to make the best of work and all practical possibilities. With a sudden transformation you can get yourself right back on form and making use of your energy. There isn't much time left to do those final things that are necessary ahead of the festive season, and you might even decide to attempt them all at the same time!

23 WEDNESDAY   *Moon Age Day 7   Moon Sign Pisces*

Look out for a period of advancement in some way. Perhaps you have made a favourable impression at work, or have achieved a bonus that you didn't expect. Whatever happens today, be prepared to take things in your stride and react very quickly to changing circumstances. An ideal day to seek out people from the past.

24 THURSDAY   *Moon Age Day 8   Moon Sign Pisces*

Trends suggest you could be in too much of a hurry today. The real pleasure in Christmas Eve lies in working hard for some of the time, but it's also worth ensuring there are intimate moments spent with those who are special to you. It shouldn't be hard for you to get into the swing of Christmas, even if you start late in the day.

25 FRIDAY
Moon Age Day 9   Moon Sign Aries

Christmas Day offers the chance to do well at social gatherings and to be the life and soul of the party. Even if you have to be pleasant to people you don't care for very much, you should do better than you expect, and can make sure that the fountain of love you shower in the direction of family members is well received and returned.

26 SATURDAY
Moon Age Day 10   Moon Sign Aries

Widening your horizons as much as possible is what today is about. It's worth having a good look at all those presents, since there may well be something in your stocking that turns out to be especially significant. There is much to be said for taking a journey today, but preferably not on your own.

27 SUNDAY
Moon Age Day 11   Moon Sign Taurus

A day to weigh up the balance between family commitments and the need to do something just for yourself. If you are certain you have fulfilled your obligations then you can afford to be slightly selfish today – though it may not turn out that way. You needn't be too influenced at the moment by what other people expect of you.

28 MONDAY
Moon Age Day 12   Moon Sign Taurus

Mars remains in your solar first house, and so just when it seems as though you might be running out of steam you can suddenly energise yourself again and also be quite forceful. Some of you might be itching to get back into harness and to be able to make an impression on life again, but for others, Christmas must run its social course.

29 TUESDAY
Moon Age Day 13   Moon Sign Taurus

You can now gain from teamwork and also from social issues, though the dominant side of your nature is still highlighted. Nobody should be particularly surprised about this because it is, after all, what is expected from a Lion. At the same time your strength lies in being honourable and willing to admit when you are wrong.

30 WEDNESDAY   *Moon Age Day 14   Moon Sign Gemini*

The Sun is now firmly ensconced in your solar sixth house and though it is a useful influence when it comes to getting things organised, you can still afford time to break from normal routines and to contribute to any upcoming New Year celebrations. A day to split your time between the practical and the specifically social.

31 THURSDAY   *Moon Age Day 15   Moon Sign Gemini*

Dynamic to the last beat of the old year, that first-house Mars pushes you on towards the final chime tonight. In fact it has potential to help you out long after midnight comes, and well into the New Year. If having both your family and your best friends around you tonight is important, arranging this in advance is essential.

RISING SIGNS FOR LEO

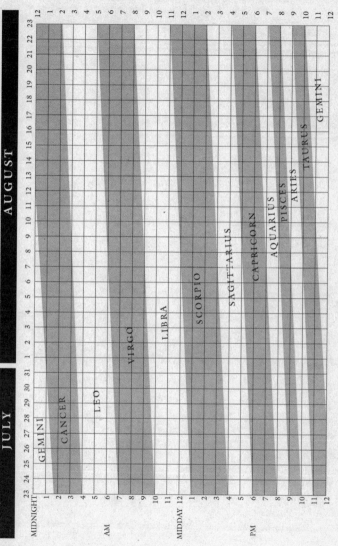

THE ZODIAC, PLANETS AND CORRESPONDENCES

The Earth revolves around the Sun once every calendar year, so when viewed from Earth the Sun appears in a different part of the sky as the year progresses. In astrology, these parts of the sky are divided into the signs of the zodiac and this means that the signs are organised in a circle. The circle begins with Aries and ends with Pisces.

Taking the zodiac sign as a starting point, astrologers then work with all the positions of planets, stars and many other factors to calculate horoscopes and birth charts and tell us what the stars have in store for us.

The table below shows the planets and Elements for each of the signs of the zodiac. Each sign belongs to one of the four Elements: Fire, Air, Earth or Water. Fire signs are creative and enthusiastic; Air signs are mentally active and thoughtful; Earth signs are constructive and practical; Water signs are emotional and have strong feelings.

It also shows the metals and gemstones associated with, or corresponding with, each sign. The correspondence is made when a metal or stone possesses properties that are held in common with a particular sign of the zodiac.

Finally, the table shows the opposite of each star sign – this is the opposite sign in the astrological circle.

Placed	Sign	Symbol	Element	Planet	Metal	Stone	Opposite
1	Aries	Ram	Fire	Mars	Iron	Bloodstone	Libra
2	Taurus	Bull	Earth	Venus	Copper	Sapphire	Scorpio
3	Gemini	Twins	Air	Mercury	Mercury	Tiger's Eye	Sagittarius
4	Cancer	Crab	Water	Moon	Silver	Pearl	Capricorn
5	Leo	Lion	Fire	Sun	Gold	Ruby	Aquarius
6	Virgo	Maiden	Earth	Mercury	Mercury	Sardonyx	Pisces
7	Libra	Scales	Air	Venus	Copper	Sapphire	Aries
8	Scorpio	Scorpion	Water	Pluto	Plutonium	Jasper	Taurus
9	Sagittarius	Archer	Fire	Jupiter	Tin	Topaz	Gemini
10	Capricorn	Goat	Earth	Saturn	Lead	Black Onyx	Cancer
11	Aquarius	Waterbearer	Air	Uranus	Uranium	Amethyst	Leo
12	Pisces	Fishes	Water	Neptune	Tin	Moonstone	Virgo